John Keble

**Letters of spiritual counsel and guidance**

John Keble

**Letters of spiritual counsel and guidance**

ISBN/EAN: 9783742816634

Manufactured in Europe, USA, Canada, Australia, Japa

Cover: Foto ©Thomas Meinert / pixelio.de

Manufactured and distributed by brebook publishing software
(www.brebook.com)

John Keble

**Letters of spiritual counsel and guidance**

# LETTERS

BY THE LATE

## REV. J. KEBLE, M.A.

# LETTERS

## OF

# SPIRITUAL COUNSEL AND GUIDANCE,

### BY THE LATE

## REV. J. KEBLE, M.A.

#### VICAR OF HURSLEY.

### Edited by

## R. F. WILSON, M.A.

#### VICAR OF ROWNHAMS, PREBENDARY OF SARUM, AND EXAMINING CHAPLAIN TO THE BISHOP OF SALISBURY.

———◆———

"Behold, thou hast instructed many, and thou hast strengthened the weak hands.
"Thy words have upholden him that was falling, and thou
hast strengthened the feeble knees."—Job iv. 3, 4.

*SECOND EDITION.*

## OXFORD and LONDON:

## JAMES PARKER AND CO.

### 1870.

" Thy Book I love because Thyself is there."

*I. Williams'* " *Thoughts in Past Years.*"

# PREFACE.

THESE Letters form no part of Keble's General Correspondence, which yet remains to be published. Materials for it had been collected, and the work begun by a far more competent Editor; but, when he was called to fill the place of one whose memory will long be held in affectionate veneration, not only in his own diocese, but throughout the Church of England, Dr. Moberly felt that the calls upon his time and thoughts would be too weighty and manifold to allow of his continuing the work. At the request of the Keble family, it was undertaken by the present Editor, and the Letters, then in Dr. Moberly's possession, were, with the consent of those who had furnished them, transferred to his hands.

These, with others which have been since contributed, are so numerous, and various in

character, and spread over so many years,
that the selecting and arranging is a work of
difficulty, and will require a considerable time
before a collection can be ready for publication.

But long before the Editor had any reason
to expect that this charge would be laid upon
him, a large number of the Letters in this
volume had been entrusted to him, on the
express understanding, that, if printed at all,
they should be in a separate collection, apart
from the General Correspondence. Many more
have since been added, on the same condition,
and the publication kindly allowed, (often at
the expense of personal feelings,) with the
charitable desire to make others, in some
measure, partakers in the benefit and comfort
which those to whom they were written had
themselves derived from them.

The Editor desires to express his sincere
thanks to all, who have contributed materials
to this collection, but most particularly to those
who, for the love of others' souls, have been
willing to place letters of so private a kind
(and to them so very precious), in the hands

of a stranger, and to entrust the use of them
to his discretion. He earnestly hopes that
nothing in his manner of dealing with them
will cause any to regret the trust thus re-
posed.

Those who are acquainted with the *Lettres
Spirituelles* of Fenelon and of S. Francis de
Sales, may trace a resemblance to them, especially to those of the saintly Bishop of Geneva,
in the Letters in this volume.

The reader must not expect to find in them
an orderly, systematic, or exhaustive treatment
of the subjects to which they refer. They
are very far from this. Written often hastily,
amid the pressure of other duties, they are, in
some cases, spontaneous effusions, prompted by
affection and sympathy for those in trouble;
but, for the most part, they were called forth
by enquiries on various matters, more or less
closely touching the spiritual life, addressed to
him by different persons, of different characters,
and under different circumstances; and they
are directed simply to the need of the particular soul. It is the special case before him

which is in the writer's mind, and not any theological handling of the points referred to. In many cases, moreover, they are the more brief and unsystematic, because he counted on supplementing them by personal advice and direction.

The collection extends over nearly fifty years : the date of the earliest letter contained in it is 1817, that of the latest 1865. As a general rule it has been thought best not to give the date of each letter, in order, as far as possible, to avoid everything which might afford a clue to the person addressed. In some cases, where there seemed no need to guard against this danger, the dates have been given.

A few Letters have been admitted into this volume which have strictly no place among Letters of Spiritual Counsel and Guidance ; such are Nos. I., II., XIX., CXIII., CXVII., CXX., CXXI., and CXXII. The two first are introduced as a beautiful and instructive example of his way of dealing *with himself ;* the others have been added, as containing, each in their several ways, some word of helpful guidance or soothing comfort amid the perplexing questions of our day.

Of the first twelve letters, a few were written before 1820, the rest, with one exception, before 1830. Letter XIII. is dated 1860, and is placed next to the one immediately preceding, as affording a remarkable illustration of the identity of his views on the subject of which these letters treat, though they were written at such a long interval.

The Letters from No. XIV. to LVIII. were all written between the years 1840 and 1850. The rest, for the most part, later. Six of the Letters in this volume have already appeared in Sir J. Coleridge's Memoir, viz. Nos. I., III., V., XI., XIX., and CVII.

This is not the occasion for remarking upon any peculiarities or graces in John Keble's character ; but there is one, which has so much to do with a right understanding of what he says, and of his manner of saying it, particularly in giving advice or direction, that it is desirable to notice it, though at some length.

When you consult a person confidentially, or hear his mind on a subject of importance, it is well to know whether there is any peculiarity in his words or manner, which is very different from what you meet with in other men. If such there be, and you are not aware of it, and do not bear it in mind, there is a risk of your mistaking the force of the advice given, or of the judgment expressed. Now, no one can fail to remark in these Letters (still more will the idea be familiar, if they had any intimate acquaintance with Keble,) the great diffidence and humility with which his advice is offered : it amounts not unfrequently to an appearance of uncertainty about the advice given ; and that, in some cases, when you would have expected that his mind would have been clearly and decidedly expressed ; or when, if you knew his life, you would know that practically as regarded himself there was no kind of uncertainty or hesitation.

It is quite possible that in this exceeding backwardness and self-distrust there may have

been some admixture of timidity, or other natural imperfection; but it chiefly arose from
that most rare humility and self-depreciation,
which had become so ingrained in all he did
and said as to be part of his very self. You
could hardly ask his opinion on a matter of any
difficulty, on which his advice would not be
given with this sort of hesitancy; so much so,
as sometimes to leave persons uncertain what
he really meant to counsel or direct, or whether he had made up his own mind in the
matter. But this conclusion would have been
entirely mistaken. With him, " I think," " I
suppose," " I believe," and other such paren-
thetical expressions of uncertainty, did not
rightly convey doubt on his own part about
the matter, so much as the habitual uprising
thought, "who was he, that he should advise
anybody?" and that the particular person who
was seeking his counsel or direction, was in
truth fitter to give it to, than to receive it
from, him. His own mind might be clear, so
that in acting himself, he would not make a
moment's hesitation : though, in determining

for another, this scrupulousness could not be restrained from utterance. Hence, with him in advising, " I think," " I suppose," must often be regarded as mere expletives. They were introduced where another, who practically saw his way with the same distinctness, would not have thought of interposing them. " I think you had better," would be rightly interpreted, "you ought:" " Don't you think it would be right ?" would be equivalent to a simple direction.

But to understand his mind and manner we must go deeper still. This manner resulted not simply from most rare personal humility : there was another element underlying and prompting this humility,—a deep sense of personal unworthiness and sinfulness, finding utterance sometimes in expressions of self-abasement and self-condemnation, so strong, as quite to startle and distress one.

Thus he writes to his dear friend, Sir J. Coleridge :—

" It really makes one afraid and ashamed to think of one's own (now 70) years of uninterrupted health,

along with the sufferings of so many persons so unlike oneself. It would be a charity if people would
sometimes in their Litanies pray for the *very* healthy,
*very* prosperous, *very* light-hearted, *very much* be-
praised," &c.—*Keble's Memoir*, p. 459.

And again, with still more startling distinctness :—

" Well can I understand from what I see in others,
and a great deal too well from myself, the heart-deep
truth of every word you say on the matter of those
sermons of Pusey's on 'Sin and Love:' they are
two great depths, too deep by far for our sounding.
I suppose our safest prayer would be, that we may
be led gradually on to the perception of where we
are, in respect both of one and the other, and not
permitted to dwell on either exclusively. For myself, my inward history is a most shameful and miserable one,—*really* quite different from what you and
others imagine ; so that I am quite sure, if you knew
it, you would be startled at the thought of coming
to such an adviser, so long and so late has the
misery been ; and it ought to be a bitter penance to
me to be so consulted. But I believe that I have
sinned before now, in drawing back on such occasions, and I hope never to do so again ; use me,
therefore, dear friend, such as I am, if I can be of
any use to you at any time ; but pray for me, *bonâ*

*fide,* that I may be contrite, for that is what I really
need."—*Keble's Memoir,* p. 326.

But even this gives an inadequate idea of
how inseparable from him this feeling was.
Here is a little note to the present Bishop of
S. Andrew's, much his junior, then Second
Master of Winchester College, with whom, at
that time, judging from the *Mr.* Wordsworth
at the end, he did not feel in very close intimacy.   It is an acknowledgment of a Translation of Mr. Keble's Morning and Evening
Hymns into Latin Sapphics, with a short
Dedication expressive of his respect and veneration for the author [a].

[a] The Bishop of S. Andrew's, in a letter to the " Guardian "
of June 8, kindly pointed out the Editor's mistake in supposing
Mr. Keble's note to be in acknowledgment of his Sermon on
Repentance.   It is hoped the Bishop will not grudge the opportunity of inserting here his graceful Dedication which gave
occasion to Mr. Keble's note.   Translation would spoil it.
So the reader must have this supplied elsewhere.   It is as
follows :—

AUCTORI INTERPRES S.P.D.

Hunc, Vates, tibi qui peperisti, Sancte, libellum
    (Tu, bonus, accipias !) doque, dicoque tuum ;
Id metuens unum ;—ne magni degener ortûs,
    Cum malè reddiderim, cœperit esse meus.

The true occasion of Mr. Keble's note thus supplied, seems

"HURSLEY VICARAGE,
*Dec.* 22, 1845.

"MY DEAR FRIEND,

"Indeed I am very much obliged by your kind present : although I have, alas! more and sadder reasons than you know, or can possibly guess, for feeling most deeply humbled at the credit which I seem most deceitfully to allow my friends to give me. I have not yet had time to read your kind present attentively, but I am sure I shall very much like it, when I do, except for the reason I have indicated. May I ask one favour more of you, which *pray* grant in the very terms in which it is asked : that you will beg that I may be truly humbled and ashamed by undeserved praise and good opinion ; I assure you, never had man more need of such a prayer.

"Ever, dear Mr. Wordsworth,
"Your obliged and affectionate
"J. KEBLE."

only to bring into stronger light, how habitually with him the eye of self-reproof was turned within. The grave subject of Repentance might seem naturally to waken up this glance. But with him even praise became a discipline of humiliation.

To quote his own words on this subject :—

"Let us check our high thoughts, and the pleasure we are apt to find in being praised, with the recollection of those faults of our own, which we know, and God knows, but which we should least wish man to know. Let that remembrance hang heavy on our hearts and prevent us from ever again feeling gay and delighted, when our brethren praise us."

Most persons of real earnestness occasionally
feel the truth, and literal suitableness of such
expressions, as applied to themselves, with an
almost overpowering clearness and force.   The
deeper the insight into the greatness and
holiness of God, and His countless mercies
towards us, the more intense and entire will
be the sense of sinfulness and unworthiness.
All earnest believers feel this sometimes.   But
it is a singular gift of grace when this feeling
is habitual; so habitual as to impress its mark
on a man's whole moral bearing, in words and
actions.   This was eminently the case with
John Keble.   Some quotations have been made
from letters, marking the depth and irrepressible strength of this feeling in his later years.
Utterance was a relief, from a sense of hypocrisy if he did not speak.   "While I held
my tongue, my bones consumed away through
my daily complaining."   How early, and how
strongly this conviction was inwrought in him,
may be seen from the following extract from
a Sermon written in 1816, at the age of twenty-
four :—

"Let us begin at the root of the evil, our hearts, by a strict judgment of ourselves, according to the rule which Christ has given us, and by earnest prayer to judge aright; let us make ourselves thoroughly sure of our own utter unworthiness, and then set ourselves in earnest to do all our own duty; so shall we have little time left to search out other men's faults. Let us resolve from this moment to think the best we can of them, and never, as we hope to stand in the last judgment, never make their doings a standard whereby to try our own, except it be to shame ourselves for not better following their good example. Whenever we feel the old leaven working within us, whenever we catch ourselves in so much as a severe thought, let us instantly fly to prayer: let us silence the unmerciful spirit by the remembrance of what God has forgiven us, and let us beat down the proud spirit with the terrors of the judgment to come."

Such an habitual estimate of self as is expressed in these and like passages, does not need explanation. It is not a weakness, but a grace. The counterpart of the language is to be found in the mouths of the chiefest of God's Saints. Let any one single out from the Bible the names of those who were specially in favour with God. Foremost among them would be the names of Abraham, Job,

David, Daniel, S. Paul, seeing that each of
these has his own special title of honour from
God Himself, in token of His favour. "The
friend of God," "the perfect man and upright,"
"the man after God's own heart," "the man
greatly beloved," "a chosen vessel unto Me."
And how do these holy persons, concerning
whom it may be said in a very special manner,
"whose praise is not of men, but of God," how
do they speak about themselves? "Who am
but dust and ashes:" "I repent and abhor
myself in dust and ashes:" "My sins are more
in number than the hairs of my head, and my
heart hath failed me:" "Oh! remember not
the sins and offences of my youth:" (and what
a blameless youth!) "We have sinned . . . . to
us belongeth confusion of face:" "Sinners, of
whom I am chief." It is to be observed, that
these are not merely expressions of humility,
but of shame and sorrow, and of conscious
sinfulness and unworthiness. They are not
merely the expression of awe at the Majesty
and Holiness of the great God with whom we
have to do, but of a sense of a depth of evil

within. In every age God's Saints have given
utterance to their feelings about themselves
in language of this sort, and with like strength
and energy. Words of deepest self-condemnation are the vernacular tongue of Saints.
It is not for the strength or character of the
expressions, that we go to Scripture. They
may be found everywhere. But it is because,
in the Scripture examples mentioned, we have
not only the expression of the feeling on one
side, but also, on the other, the word of God's
approval of those who so esteemed and spoke
of themselves. The words, as regards themselves, are the words of man, but the judgment
is the judgment of God. And those whose
habitual estimate of themselves most nearly
corresponds with the literal sense of the words
of those holy men of old, will, so far, more
nearly approach to their likeness, who "had
this testimony, that they pleased God."

It might seem sufficient thus to have pointed
out, that this vivid present consciousness of
personal sinfulness is a characteristic of God's
choicest Saints. It would be natural, and it

may be, more becoming, thus to leave the subject. But to do so, would be to miss a chief
part in the lesson of the life of him who
speaks in these Letters; for, in truth, the real
reason why such words seem to many, perhaps to most persons, either to savour of ex-
aggeration, or else to betoken a conscience
burdened with the memory of grievous sin, is
to be found in the low and insufficient estimate of the awful heinousness and deadly evil
of *all* sin, too commonly prevailing in the
thoughts even of earnest and devout persons.
Those who have not realized and inwrought
into their minds some idea of the inconceivable and unapproachable holiness of Him with
Whom we have to do, and of the awful near-
ness of His indwelling Presence in our souls,
can never duly estimate the presumptuous
guilt of sins of thought. The following extract will shew what John Keble's teaching
was on this subject :—

" Let our subject to-day be, The One Holy Spirit,
with His differing gifts, abiding alike in every mem-
ber of Christ.

" Consider what a fearful notion this gives us of
our condition. To know that we are in God's sight,
that He looks on our heart, is exceeding awful: to
know that He looks on us as persons whom He has
called to be His own, whom He bought with His
own Blood, and for whom, therefore, He cares with
especial care, this makes our case still more serious:
but to be aware that the Most High and Holy Spirit,
by the covenant of our Baptism, is really abiding
within us: that we are, as S. Paul said, the Temple
of God, and that the Spirit of God dwelleth in us:
this, indeed, is awful beyond all awfulness. How
can we be idle, thoughtless, negligent of our souls?
how can we deal lightly with any duty? above all,
how can we pollute our souls and bodies with any
kind of wilful sin? we, to whom Christ has said, 'I
will pray the Father, and He shall give you another
Comforter, and He shall abide with you for ever[a].'"

How entirely the view which he thus
brings before others pervaded his own mind,
and gave a tone and colour to all his
thoughts about himself, we have ample means
of knowing.

Those who have read his Lectures on
Poetry, will remember his theory, that Poetry

[a] Plain Sermons, by contributors to the "Tracts for the
Times," No. CLXXVIII.

is the irrepressible expression of pent-up feelings, which crave for utterance, and yet are
too deep for any more familiar interchange
or expression. Poetry (according to Keble)
is the pouring out of the most sacred utterances of the soul; relieving the spirit of
thoughts which it shrinks from communicating
to another, and yet which are a burden till
they have thus in some way taken shape and
clothed themselves in words. Poetry becomes
a sort of public confession of what is within,
though veiled by being generalized. The
Poet speaks his own thoughts, his own feelings, his own troubles and inner griefs, but
he puts them as it were into the mouth of
another, and so finds relief.

Bearing in mind this his theory of Poetry,
his poetical utterances come to have more or
less the character of Confessions [b]; indeed, it
might, perhaps, be not untrue to say, that
the "Christian Year" was to John Keble, in

---

[b] "I had long ago considered about printing the Dedication
you speak of: but somehow or other (though Davison recommended it), I could not bring myself to it; it seemed too
much like printing one's own private Confessions: *and so to
be sure is half the book."—Coleridge's Memoir*, p. 121.

some measure, what the Confessions of S. Augustine were to that great Saint.

Looking at it in this light, let any one take up the book, turn to any of those well-known passages which express deepest self-condemnation and abasement, and see what is the nature of the sin which weighed so heavily upon his spirit. It will be found, in every case, to be sins of thought; shortcomings and imperfections in faith, gratitude, love, or devotion; wandering imaginations, unchastened desires. Sins about which, it is to be feared, most Christians hardly give themselves any concern at all, and for which they certainly do not judge themselves very severely.

Take as an example those stanzas of the Poem for the Sixth Sunday after Trinity :—

> " If ever, floating from faint earthly lyre,
> Was wafted to your heart one high desire,
>    By all the trembling hope ye feel,
>    Think on the minstrel as ye kneel :

> " Think on the shame, that dreadful hour
>       When tears shall have no power,
>    Should his own lay th' accuser prove,
>    Cold while he kindled others' love :

And let your prayer for charity arise,
That his own heart may hear his melodies,
     And a true voice to him may cry,
   ' Thy GOD forgives—thou shalt not die.' "

What is it which he fears may bring shame upon him in the Day of Judgment, and make "his own lay" his accuser, and against which he so earnestly desires the prayers of others? It is coldness and unlove.

     " Cold while he kindled others' love."

Or take again the verses for the Twenty-fourth Sunday after Trinity :—

" Or what if Heaven for once its searching light
     Lent to some partial eye, disclosing all
The rude bad thoughts, that in our bosom's night
     Wander at large, nor heed Love's gentle thrall?

" Who would not shun the dreary uncouth place?
     As if, fond leaning where her infant slept,
A mother's arm a serpent should embrace :
     So might we friendless live, and die unwept."

Here to live friendless and die unwept, and to be a cause of shuddering horror to others, such as a serpent would be to a mother, if found coiled in her infant's cradle,—

all this is the result of no deadly act or even word of sin; but it rises before him as the natural and inevitable consequence which *must* follow, if, for one moment, the softening veil were withdrawn, and our "*rude bad thoughts*" exposed to the eyes of our friends.

Another most striking instance may be found in the Poem for the Seventeenth Sunday after Trinity, where love of pleasure, desire for the praise of man, or fretfulness and discontent, are set forth as sins which as far surpass in guilt the crimes and idolatries of the Jews, as Heaven is above earth, and

"As earthly hopes abused, are less than hopes divine."

And why? A few lines further on we read,

"Thou Who hast deigned the Christian's heart to call Thy Church and Shrine."

This is the thought; it is this living faith in, and continual remembrance of, the indwelling Presence, which causes such sins to appear to him so exceeding sinful, such an outrage against the majesty and condescending love of Almighty God.

Many other examples might be given, but these must suffice ; the thought once suggested, can hardly fail to rise up again and again, to those who are familiar with his Poems [c].

It cannot be matter for surprise, that one thus penetrated with a sense of his own unworthiness, should have shrunk at times from the discharge of that special office which, after being for long in abeyance in our branch of the Church, has lately (through the grace of God stirring men's hearts to seek after a deeper and more thorough repentance) been called for, and claimed by our people at our hands, in a manner which leaves us no choice.

None more than he, felt the loss which the disuse of Confession has brought upon our Church, or rejoiced more in its growing restoration ; but to his deep humility it would have been a relief, if penitents could have

[c] See " Christian Year," First Sunday after Christmas, Monday before Easter, Good Friday, First Sunday after Easter, Second, Third, and Twelfth Sunday after Trinity, &c.

See also " Lyra Innocentium," Prefatory Poem, Danger of Praise, &c., &c.

been led to seek it from other hands and lips than his own.

This feeling, too, finds vent and utterance in the "Christian Year:" we see it in his Poem on the Visitation of the Sick :—

> "Such have I seen: and as they pour'd
> Their hearts in every contrite word,
> How have I rather long'd to kneel
> And ask of them sweet pardon's seal !"

Nor was this only the feeling of youth and inexperience when first called upon thus to exercise his sacred office: to the end of his life it remained the same, or rather deepened in him; and "the grey-haired saint" of threescore years and ten, who had fought a good fight, and kept the faith, and well-nigh finished his course, to whom eyes turned, and hearts clung, wherever throughout the world, children of the English Church were to be found, shrank with the same deep consciousness of unfitness and unworthiness from the exercise of the "authority committed unto" him, as did the young Priest in the early days of his ministry. Those who have been

privileged to receive such ministrations at his
hands, well know how, as it were in spite of
himself, this feeling impressed itself on all
his outward bearing.

And here lay the secret of that exceeding
tenderness to others, which was in him almost as striking a characteristic as his severity
towards himself.   It is ever thus.   He who
is most deeply penetrated with the thought
of his own sin, will ever think most tenderly
of the failings of others.   His deep sense of
the holiness of God, will indeed make him
hate sin, in himself or in others, with an
intensity of hatred unknown to the less pure
in heart; but though he " hate [d] the trespass
most, yet when all other love is lost," he will
"love the poor sinner," after the pattern of
Him, Who, though understanding the sinfulness of sin as none other could possibly understand it, yet never drew back from any, how
deeply stained soever with deadly sin; Who
Himself gives contrition, and then accepts it,

[d] " Christian Year," Second Sunday after Trinity.

and "shrinks not at our sin-defiled touch, but accounts our penitence as innocence, and our grief for our sins as purity<sup>c</sup>."

In conclusion, a few words of apology are due for the length of this Preface.

It seemed to the Editor that, without some discussion of the subject, readers who had not personally known him, might be perplexed by passages in the Letters, or, it may be, led to erroneous surmises; and in truth also it has been a relief to himself, thus to give utterance to some of his thoughts about the beloved and honoured writer, and to endeavour, however faintly and imperfectly, to sketch, and so bring before others, that one special feature, in which the grace of God shone forth most markedly, in the saintly character of him with whom it was his privilege to live in very close intimacy for thirty years: to whom he owes a vast debt, a debt not only of love and kindness undeserved and unvary-

* See "Sermons preached at Consecration of S. Saviour's, Leeds." Sermon I.

ing throughout those thirty years, but also another, and a far deeper one,—a debt which (so be it) may, perhaps, be truly expressed in the words of the aged Apostle to his son in the faith—

ὅτι καὶ σεαυτόν μοι προσοφείλεις.

R. F. W.

Rownhams, Southampton,
S. Mark's Day, 1870.

# CONTENTS.

c

PAGE

CVI. Oversights not to be brooded over . . . 192

CVII. Sadness in Devotion not always wrong . . ib.

CVIII. To a Gentleman who had Consulted him about a Change
of Profession, and taking Holy Orders . . 194

CIX. On Self-denial . . . . . 195

CX. Against Despondency in respect to one's Prayers . 197

CXI. On Joining an Association for United Prayer . . 199

CXII. On Disinclination to Prayer . . . . 200

CXIII. To One on the Eve of his Ordination . . . 204

CXIV. A Word on the Study of the Fathers . . . 205

CXV. Sacramental Confession not to be of Single Sins only . 206

CXVI. On the Presence of Non-Communicants at the Holy
Eucharist . . . . . . 207

CXVII. On the Real Presence in the Holy Eucharist . . 209

CXVIII. On Reservation for Communion of the Sick . . 212

CXIX. On Celibacy as a Counsel of Perfection . 213

CXX. On Vows of Celibacy . . . . . 214

CXXI. On the Religious Revivals in Ireland . . . 215

CXXII. On the Burial Office . . . . . 223

CXXIII. On the Ritual of the Church of England . . 233

# LETTER I.

My dear ——,

. . . . I knew you would be very sorry when you heard of what has come upon us, and I feel that I can write freely to you about it: but I cannot half describe to you the depth and intensity, at least so it seemed to me, of my thoughts and feelings during M. A.'s illness, and for some time since. Certainly no loss could be so great, humanly speaking, to E. and my Father, but they are both such sort of people, that I have long been used to consider every thing that happens to them as a certain good: and there was nothing bitter in my grief as far as they were concerned ; much less in thinking of M. A. herself: but the real bitterness was when I thought of many things in which I have been far less kind to her than I ought to have been—somehow or other I have for years been accustomed to talk to her far more freely than to any body else in the world, though of course there were two or three whom I loved quite as well : but it has so happened that whenever I was moody or fretful she has had to bear with me more than any one ; and if I chose, I could sit down and torment myself by the hour with the thought of it :

B

this is the only feeling of real bitterness that I have on the subject, but I know it is wrong to indulge it, and I trust soon to get over it entirely: indeed I seem to have done so already, only I feel one cannot in any way depend upon oneself. I am certain no person who believes in the Atonement ought to indulge in bitter remorse, and therefore, by God's blessing, I don't mean to be uncomfortable if I can help it, even in the thought of my past faults. I have been so too much already, and it only serves to make one lazy, and weaken one's own hands and one's friends. If you please, therefore, don't let us encourage one another in melancholy any more, but let us always resolutely look to the bright side of things ; and among other helps to be quiet, let us always talk as freely to one another as we do now— for nothing relieves one so much as making a clean breast.

I never was so much impressed with the value and excellency of cheerfulness as a Christian virtue, as I have been since M. A.'s death. The remembrance of her peculiar cheerfulness, (for she had more of it than any of us, except perhaps my Father,) goes so far towards keeping us all up, especially E. We keep thinking how vexed she would be to see us annoying ourselves about her, and how she always wanted every body to live in sunshine, and it quite makes us ashamed and afraid to feel desolate. You may easily imagine what a support this is,

to E., whose thoughts, both from her temper and circumstances, are more entirely fixed on M. A. than
either of ours can be. Of course she must feel like
a widow, but I trust not as a desolate one: certainly
she seems alive to every comfort, and her prevalent
feeling is one of deep thankfulness for the assurance
of M. A.'s happiness. . . .

I like your plans of reading, but don't be disheartened if you seem to do little: only I would
not indulge in reveries. As you speak of good
books, do look at the life of Mr. Bonnell, if it comes
in your way. It is in the list of the Christian Knowledge Society, and Hawkins, I know, can lend it to
you,—see p. 153. There is a passage which I have
found useful, and I suspect you may too. You cannot think how often you come into my mind, especially now I am endeavouring to train myself to
a more thorough content and cheerfulness than I
ever yet practised. For I fancy that you and I require in some respects the same sort of training.
At any rate I know too well what passes in my
own mind to think any thing contemptible in you.
Now I think this is enough about ourselves, for I
hold it to be a selfish and dangerous sort of thing
for people to be always turning their eyes inward.
But don't let this hinder you from writing always as
freely of whatever is uppermost, as you do now,—
only please not to let your own faults, or any thing
uncomfortable, be often uppermost. As I said be-

fore, I am sure it is not natural it should be so, in those for whom Christ died. This lesson I have learned of dear M. A., and I hope not to forget it, but to have it perfect by the time I see her again : and if I can get you to have it too, so much the better for us all. She often used to speak of you, and I daresay to pray for you, for she fancied you not quite comfortable, and she had a great feeling for that sort of discomfort.

God bless you now, my dear Friend ; let me hear from you as often as it seems to do you any good, and don't mind what you write. Mention how your Sister is ; I have heard nothing of her for a long time.

Ever and ever yours,<br>J. K., jun.

## LETTER II.

### To another Friend, on the same Subject.

I DON'T think I ever felt the Almighty so near me, as during this whole time ; and you know when one is impressed with that feeling, it is quite impossible to repine. And another thing which has the same effect, is the strong impression how very much M. A. would be vexed if she could know that one is fretting at her deliverance. One feels it more in her case than one should in most others, because of the very remarkable cheerfulness and contentedness of her character; she quite started back from any thing like querulousness, and I trust I have made up my mind to learn of her, now she is in Paradise, what I was but too slow in learning while we had her in sight—that "all is for the best." Dear soul, I cannot help thinking her death in many respects very like that of a martyr. She had a strong impression that something was going to happen, and seemed as if she was preparing herself like a devoted being. She had subdued all her little quickness of manner I may call it rather than of temper, so that the servants remarked the change in her; could not bear to have fault found with any body or any thing, and was always overflowing with thankfulness and resignation.

If an Angel had given her notice of what was to happen she could not have prepared herself more thoroughly for it, as far as we can judge. . . . And now we have the unspeakable comfort of thinking that it is our own fault if every moment does not bring us nearer to her again. Sometimes indeed it will come across one, "What *can* E. do without her?" but it will not do to distress one's self about her, who has been so long and so kindly helped. No doubt God has ways of supporting her more than we know or dream of; and so the end is, we *must* be comfortable, if we would not be unthankful and unchristian.

# LETTER III.

## ON CONQUERING MELANCHOLY BY ACTIVE KINDNESS
## TO OTHERS.

MY DEAR ——,

I am bound to thank you over and over again for your last letter; it was and is a real comfort to me: for I am tolerably sure you are in the right way; only don't dwell too much upon whatever may have been wrong: to some minds it may be necessary, but not to those who are in danger of becoming indolent by too much thinking about themselves: and when you find yourself, as I dare say you sometimes do, overpowered as it were by melancholy, the best way is to go out, and do something kind to somebody or other.  Objects either rich or poor will generally present themselves in the hour of need to those who look for them in earnest, although Oxford is not perhaps the most convenient place to find them in.  However there they surely are if you will take the trouble of looking for them, and perhaps that very trouble is in some sort an advantage in doing away a moody fit; although I always reckon it a great privilege of a country Parson that his resources in this way lie close at his own door.

Writing, too, I have known in many cases, a very great relief, but I almost doubt the expediency of preserving journals, at least of looking much back upon them; if one could summon resolution to do so, I fancy the best way would be to write on till one was a little unburthened, and then put one's confessions in the fire. But in all these things, of course no one can judge for his neighbour. And whatever you do, don't put your confessions to *me* in the fire; for it does my heart good to receive them: it makes me hope that I am sometimes useful, which is a sensation I don't very often experience.

# LETTER IV.

### To the Same, on Resisting Inclinations to Remorse.

My very dear ——,

I cannot say I was surprised, though I was deeply grieved at your account. You know, better than I can tell you, all that I would say to comfort and support you in this very severe trial, and indeed you have said all that one ought to need by way of comfort, in what you tell me of your sister, and of —— himself: I cannot help thinking that you judge yourself too harshly in what you say, and have no doubt in my own mind, that he would give a very different account of the effect of your mutual intercourse on him. But indeed, I know too well that there is no dictating to other men's feelings in matters of this sort: only as a general rule, I should say to every one, do not indulge in remorse as a matter of feeling or fancy. There is none of us but has reason enough to make himself miserable in that way, if it were at all allowable to do so.

## LETTER V.

My dearest Friend,

It is presumptuous in me, I know, to pretend to comfort you on so sad an occasion as this, but I *must* tell you truly that my heart bleeds at the thought of your loss, though I know it is absolutely impossible for me to sympathize with you under it ; but you have better comforters who do, not only —— and dear ——, but a more effectual one than either, even Him, who when He saw a dead man carried out, the only son of his mother, had compassion on her. He is even now touched with a feeling of the sorrow of heart which has fallen upon you and your dear wife, whom God bless, confirm, and comfort for His sake.

My dear friends, think as little as you can of yourselves, but think of the blessed infant whom you presented so few days ago before Christ in His earthly temple ; think of her being even now admitted to serve Him in His heavenly temple, day and night, and knowing and praising Him infinitely better than the greatest saint on earth can do ; and though it is nothing in comparison of Eternity, yet it is blessing enough to assuage your grief,—which, however good and Christian, must confess itself to be but earthly,—when you consider that your darling is put into her Saviour's arms so many years before the time that most of His servants are admitted there, *quite* safe, *quite* good, *quite* happy, and I dare to say it, overflowing with love for you beyond what all your kindness and tenderness could have made her comprehend in the longest life that parents and children can expect to enjoy together here. And although David said his child could not return to him, yet since we are taught that there is a sympathy between Paradise and earth, at least between the saints in one, and the saints in the other, what if Christian parents by holy living, should be supposed to have this comfort among others, that their lost children still watch over them, or in some way or other know of their well doing ? The thought is not, I am persuaded, unscriptural, but thank God you have no need of it. " For if we believe that Jesus died and rose again, even so them also which sleep in Jesus will God bring with Him." You need not look further for comfort than these words.

May He in Whom alone we can know comfort, make them, and all other consolations which His

Providence has in store for you, so truly comfortable to you, that you shall be able to look backward even to this sad time with humble thankfulness to Him for helping you to suffer as Christians. So prays, from the bottom of his heart,

Your affectionate friend,

1820. J. KEBLE.

## LETTER VI.

### To a College Friend, on Changing his Profession.

My very dear Friend,

. . . . We are not, God be thanked, in our own hands, but in the hands of One Who loves us infinitely better than we do ourselves : if we could but once possess ourselves with that belief (which yet is more certain than any thing which we do not see with our own eyes), how little, comparatively, would such trials as these appear to us, in comparison, I mean, with the least sin. And yet we commit great sins every day as if they were things of course. Indeed, we all need one another's prayers very much, but not always in those respects most, in which our friends are apt to suppose we need them most. How comfortable to think that there is one Friend from whom none of our necessities can be hid, and who cares for them all, if we have not wilfully rejected His care.

I am sure I need not apologize for writing in this strain to you, who are so possessed, as I trust, with the love of our dear Master, that you would be glad to dedicate yourself entirely to His more especial Service and Ministry. But persevere with a good heart, my dear fellow, where you are, and do not doubt that Providence will give you opportunities enough of being useful.

And perhaps to any man, who would fain be in the clerical profession, but is hindered by circumstances, it may not be amiss to consider, that if the chance of doing good is increased, the responsibility is increased along with it: and it is a fearful thing to think that one owes a heavier debt than one's fellows to the Great Owner of all. Aye, so fearful, that nothing could enable one to support the thought, except it were the same recollection with which I ended the last paragraph, and with which, if we brought it in as often as we have occasion, we should end every paragraph and every sentence which we write or speak, i.e. that we have One who has redeemed our infinite debt, as well as promised us unfailing supplies for the future.

1819.

# LETTER VII.

### To the Same, on the same Subject.

My very dear Friend,

. . . . I know very well what those involuntary scruples and doubtings are, which you say oppress you so sorely. I dare say, indeed I see by your letter, that you take the right view of the matter, and use the right means,—Prayer *and constant endeavours to improve in all other parts of holy living*, to cure, or at least abate the infirmity. I wish if you have not done it yet, you would read a Sermon of dear good old Richard, "On the Certainty and Perpetuity of Faith in the Elect[a]," with a view to your own case. I have been looking it over this morning, and do not see what can be wanting to a man's consolation, who being distressed like you, shall thoroughly and Christianly consider that Sermon. It is not Calvinistic, at least in any unpleasant sense of the word, so do not be frightened at its title.

As to your profession, I think you were, and are, quite in the right to let your friends choose for you, what way you had best regulate your worldly interests. As they, I verily believe, care more about your getting rich than you do yourself, they are

* Hooker, vol. iii. part ii. Oxf. Ed.

likely to manage better for you : and in the meanwhile, you have so much the more leisure for thoughts
and studies which you like better ; provided always,
that your said friends do not love you quite well
enough to pick pockets, or sic like, in your behalf.

As to your not being a Clergyman, I am inclined
to think that on the whole, the law of compensation
is observed pretty exactly in the distribution of the
cares and consolations of the different professions ;
and though a Layman who is indeed a Christian,
has not so much leisure for the direct exercise of
devotion, &c., he has the great comfort of knowing
that his example is more likely to do good, as it is
less likely to be misinterpreted as the result of
worldly motives, or the mere cant of a profession :
a thought which I often fancy I can detect darting
itself into people's minds, and hindering them from
minding what we say to them. In short, my dear
——, you would, I am satisfied, if you were now to
change, and become one of us, find anxieties and
annoyances quite enough, temporally speaking, to
overbalance any increase of comfort. If we do not,
it is, I am afraid, because we are not considerate
enough about the unspeakable awefulness of our trust,
and are therefore too soon satisfied with ourselves :
or else because we do not rate what God requires
of Christian people high enough, and therefore are
too soon satisfied with our flocks. So, unless you
think that you cannot be as good a Christian in your

present profession as in ours, or in any other, I advise you to stifle all these regrets, and work on con-
tentedly in your present line ; and I doubt not of
a time coming, in which you will even rejoice (strange
as it may seem to you now) that you were not a
Parson.

## LETTER VIII.

### To a Friend, on the Strictness of our Lord's Teaching in the Gospel.

MY DEAR FRIEND,

You see already what an unworthy choice of an
adviser you have made, by my long delay in answering your very kind letter; which affected me
a good deal in various ways, and not least with
shame at finding myself, as without foolish affecta-
tion I really did, so utterly unprepared and unworthy
to be so trusted.  I thought I would give myself
a little time to think over the points mentioned in
your letter.  But in so scrambling and dissipated
a way does one proceed, that I fear I have not
thought to any good purpose of the first, and shall
write no better an answer now, than I should have
done the hour after I received it: as to the second,
all the time I can spare . . . . has been long devoted
to thinking of it.  And as it is so much more important of the two, and if I mistake not involves the
answer to the other in it, I will speak to it first.

The plain truth then is, my dear friend, that I have no doubt whatever, that the misgivings you feel about the great strictness of the Gospel precepts —of our Saviour's advice more particularly—are perfectly right and reasonable—and the more you allow them, *in a quiet way*, to influence you in practice, the happier and wiser you will be. It is nothing in the world, I am almost certain, but the great degeneracy of the Christian Church (foretold in the Scriptures as plainly as possible) which makes people turn away from certain precepts as if they were too strict to be practised, and have recourse to so many poor miserable shifts to get rid of them. And I think, as a general rule, one of the best remedies for this would be to consider these commandments as so many instances of *friendly advice*, rather than as so many tasks set us—not to deal with them as conditions, arbitrarily appointed before one shall be allowed to enter into heaven, but as practices and tempers of mind, naturally and reasonably flowing from what we know to be the truth of our condition, and of God's dealings with us. For instance, when the question is about such a precept as St. Matt. xix. 21, we are not to be nicely enquiring, how much money is to be given in alms, but we are to consider whether it is not natural and reasonable for one, who sincerely believes the Gospel, to lay out every farthing in some way, which deserves to be called alms, i.e. in providing for the reasonable wants of

others rather than his own superfluities, however
innocent in themselves these latter may be.  It is
much better, as far as I can judge, on many accounts,
to ask ourselves rather, what is *reasonable?* than, what
is necessary?  The same may be said of humility,
forgiveness of injuries, self-denial, devotional exercises,
and indeed every part of the Christian life.  (Did
you ever read Law's " Serious Call?" or his " Christian Perfection?")  Now if one looks at things in this
light, judging always of what is reasonable and natural with a view to the next world, I allow it will
be quite impossible not to feel sorrow and shame
and fear very often, perhaps oftener than not, both
for oneself, and for those committed to one's charge.
But still this is perfectly consistent with "a cheerful
view of religion;" indeed the more cheerfully one
looks at that, the higher hopes one entertains and
the more one's heart is set upon the glorious des-
tinies in store for us, the more painful must be the
thought how sadly we have abused, and too often
are abusing or neglecting such talents.   Who so
cheerful in religion as St. Paul?  Yet he honestly
owned himself the chief of sinners in his own eyes.
Depend upon it, if a man does but try and *act up*
to these views, especially in the matter of humility—
and if he always goes upon what is reasonable, and
not upon mere feeling—indeed not at all by feeling
if he can help it—he will not want cheerfulness in
his religion, neither will he despond, however ill he

may think of things. He will be as much awake as a bold and skilful seaman in a storm, who knows how much his own safety and that of his messmates depends on his keeping up his spirits, and doing his best.

I have referred you already, in a parenthesis, to what I should think, if read very considerately, you will find the best authorities on this subject; perhaps you were acquainted with them before—in any case I should like you to look at them and let me know if they seem at all likely to *steady your thoughts* upon it. Bp. Wilson somewhere or other recommends the " Christian Perfection" very highly : probably you will see reason to think them books not to be left carelessly about, nor put into every one's hands, but I will say nothing to bias your judgment any more about them.

Now to the question about dealing with Dissenters, regularly or irregularly such. I confess I do not see how a clergyman can well wash his hands of them altogether. . . . It will always be a question of discretion and charity, to whom one should apply one's self, at any particular moment, in order to have the fairest chance of doing them good,—and Dissenters in some respects may be more impracticable, harder to be got at than most others; in this respect they may be practically, in a certain sense, excluded from one's care, but I think one would do better not to consider them as being so in theory; one would have one's eye on

them as much as one could, just as one would watch
over persons guilty of other sins, humanly speaking
incurable, I should rather say, of which one sees no
present chance of cure [b].   Of course, if this be true
of Dissenters, it is more so of those who are mere
liberalists: no doubt there are many such cases in
which it may be useful to point out the absurdity
of their conduct, and leave them to judge of it for
themselves; but it seems giving them up a great
point, to allow that one's interest in them really
ceases, because they choose to fancy you have none,
or only a partial one.

[b] The question here touched is simply, why a clergyman ought not
to look on Dissenters in his parish as entirely removed from his charge.

Elsewhere in these letters, Mr. Keble has expressed the feelings
which he entertained towards Dissenters individually, and his appre-
ciation of excellences among them.   As to the manner of dealing with
them, the few following words are from one of his Sermons:—"Nor
let it be supposed that there is any want of charity in making some
difference in your behaviour to persons, and treating them with some
reserve, because they are enemies to the Church, or in any other way
going morally wrong."—*Plain Sermons,* vol. viii. p. 121.

Nor did he lay all the guilt of separation on them, as appears from
this observation to Mr. Tyacke, Rector of St. Levan, in 1864 or 1865:
"Dissenters should be dealt with lovingly and forbearingly, as being,
alas! the wronged party in bygone times."—Quoted from a letter of
the Rev. J. S. Tyacke to the Rev. J. Frewen Moor.

But these sentiments are not inconsistent with a strong conviction
that there is sin in the separation of bodies of Christians from the
Church, in their earnest and active opposition to her, and in their ener-
getic condemnation of her doctrines and forms of worship: and that it
is the duty of a clergyman not to lose sight of this in his parish, but to
be ready to do what he can, as opportunity may serve, for bringing over
members of those bodies to the Church.—ED.

Now, my dear ——; you will say I have tolerably overlaid you with my prose, but do not act as if you thought I had done it on purpose to hinder you from writing me another nice long letter ; such letters do my heart good, they ought to do so in the best sense. I am only now about writing to H. grievously ashamed of myself. God bless you. (*N.B.* I authorize you to return this.)

1823.

Ever yⁿ affecˡʸ,
J. K.

## LETTER IX.

### To the Same.

My dear Friend,

I was a good deal ashamed of myself before, and now I have been reading once again your very kind letter, I am much more so ; but I had in some sort depended on seeing you in one of my two visits to Oxford since September, and rather wished to talk with you, than to write to you, on the very interesting subjects we have fallen upon. I doubt not before this time you have pretty well satisfied yourself about some of them, but as I know in these matters one generally goes on thinking and thinking for a very long time, and it is hardly ever too late to add to one's convictions, I shall talk of them just as if I had had your letter yesterday. With regard to Law, I thoroughly agree with you that he ought to be read with caution : first and foremost with great caution, lest one should

delight one's self so much with the ingenuity and elo-
quence of the writer as to forget that 'tis a very
practical book; this I take to be the caution most
requisite for the generality of readers. I agree with
you in not being able to go along with him in some
of his statements : but it is commonly in matters of
detail; on his general principles, I think, he hardly
leaves you any doubt.

The unity of motive which he recommends, is,
I am persuaded, the only way to be comfortable
in this world, and surely it is the Christian way
to be happy in the next ; but then as to the
best method of practising and improving one's self
in it, these as surely, must vary, I should think,
with the characters and circumstances of different
persons, so that no two human beings probably
would have to pursue, externally, the same line of
conduct, though they might go upon exactly the
same principles : and this is what Law occasionally
seems to forget, e.g. about singing Psalms, whether
you have a voice or ear, or no—to which I should
add what he says about reading Plays, which he
condemns in the lump, without even excepting
Shakespeare—and this is a good instance of the
sort of modification I should propose for Law:
he thinks things being liable to gross abuse, and
actually so perverted in general, ought to be given
up ; but query, whether they might not be taken
and applied to a higher use, sanctified as it were,

and whether this being acted on, would not prove as real a sacrifice as the other, and a safer, because more unobtrusive, kind of self-denial. Did you ever read Robert Boyle's "Occasional Reflections?" they are an instance of the sort of thing I mean, and I persuade myself St. Paul meant the same also, when he wrote about meat of various kinds, "that every creature of God is good," &c. I Tim. iv. 4, 5. What he says of various tastes in food, may be applied, I should think, to *tastes* of all sorts; one is not to destroy them, but to make them serve some good and religious purpose; perhaps the expression "living sacrifice" (Rom. xii. 1) may be meant to hint something of this sort. This sort of principle once established, there seems no necessity for condemning or allowing such and such amusements in toto; every one must be left to judge for himself, whether they suit his character and circumstances, and this will hold of clergymen as well as of other men.

You will probably have met with Bp. Horne's "Cautions to the Readers of Mr. Law," and will have found that they do not refer to the points *we* have in hand immediately: but the sad set of errors into which such a man was permitted to fall, should certainly be a caution to us how much we allow ourselves to be dazzled by his abilities, or overpowered, as it were, by his peremptory tone. We should *check* him, I think, with Bp. Wilson, and then we shall be tolerably sure to be right.

With regard to what you say of checking improper conversation, no doubt it is our duty, and must be done by each man according to his means and measure; to seem, I should say, to be, very much annoyed and *distressed* by it, would I should think, in very many cases, prove a sufficient rebuke; now and then one must speak out more decidedly. I have been greatly wanting in this amongst other duties: but once or twice, when I have made up my mind to it among strangers, I have found no reason to think I did harm or offended any body. In general, perhaps, it would be safer, and more effectual, to direct what one says on such occasions against the *folly*, rather than the *wickedness*, of what one has to complain of. But this is just one of the things, in which general rules can do least, and discretion and common sense most.

Here I have been writing away, as if I had a right to dictate or advise on points upon which I am a very young thinker, and alas! a far younger practitioner! —but you have my *theory*, and if you think it right, you will help me in my practice. There is a way of doing so which I need not name to you, and which I earnestly beg of you to employ for me.

I sincerely condole with you on the sad instance which —— tells me has occurred in your parish. It is one of those startling cases which must be looked for, from time to time, in an age of depravity and apostacy. He told me what he said to you about it, with which

I heartlily concurred. My own notion is that clergymen generally have more to blame themselves for as
to neglect in the way of example, and the way of
*special intercession,* than in the way of direct warning:
though I am afraid my own indolence and timidity
make me a bad judge rather of this matter. I would
add that what is most *shocking,* very frequently is far
from having the worst *effect.* It opens people's eyes,
sometimes, to their true state ; whereas if they had
gone on with comparative decency in the ordinary
godlessness of their neighbours, they would never
have come to a right sense of things. I hope it may
be so, sooner or later, in this instance.....

Now Farewell, and God bless you, my dear
Friend,

Ever and ever yours,

1823. J. K.

## LETTER X.

### To the Same, on the Death of his Sister.

My very dear Friend,

By some accident your letter only reached me
after post-time last night, or I would have answered
it immediately, although what can I say that you
and our dear Friend —— will not have said to yourselves over and over ? The comfort is, that the
thoughts which now support you will, by God's gracious blessing, endure, and prove inexhaustible, as all

His consolations are : they will not pass away, as
the sting of regret and sorrow, after more or less
time, is ordained by Him to pass.   What can be
a more abiding source of consolation, than the contemplation with assured hope, of a soul so remarkable for a clear and noble Christian simplicity as
your dear Sister's was (if one may without presumption affirm it of any one), passing into that region
of peace, where all is pure, noble, simple, and Christian, and welcomed thither by the myriads of kindred
spirits which are there waiting for the remainder of
those with whom they are to be made perfect ?   It
is unmixed joy: but as you say, we must not expect
to enter into it : we must submit to call the house
so visited, the house of mourning, and keenly to feel
it so : only let us try to offer up our consolations
and our sorrows together, as a sacrifice and memorial
which He may be pleased to accept ; and especially
to regard in that light the efforts, which affection
will be ever prompting us to make, in the way of
doing that which the Departed we know would most
approve.

## LETTER XI.

### To a Friend, who had consulted him on the Scruples of Another Person.

I AM clearly of opinion the young lady should
discontinue those observances which seem to fret and

distract her so much. It seems like Fasting, which no one is tied to, even by the laws of the Church, when it is *bona fide* against their health : much less by any rule they can set themselves.

Clearly this is a case of melancholy from bodily constitution, and the person should be recommended to avoid all vows and singularities of every kind, as mere snares. I seem to be speaking so positively about what I must be ignorant of, that I am afraid my opinion is worth even less than usual ; but supposing the representation in your friend's letter to be correct, and Jeremy Taylor right in his *Ductor Dubitantium*, touching the management of a scrupulous conscience, (p. 158, et seq. [e]), I don't think I can be very wide of the mark. . . . At any rate a person of this temperament should be cautioned, as matter of *duty*, to refrain from binding herself by anything like voluntary vows in future : it is a mere snare, and should be repressed like any other temp-

[e] The following are a few of the sentences, to which reference is probably made.—Ed.

"Let the scrupulous man avoid all excess in mortifications and corporal austerities, because these are apt to trouble the body, and consequently disorder the mind."

"Let the scrupulous man interest himself in as few questions of intricate dispute and minute disquisitions as he can."

"Let the scrupulous man take care that he make no vows of any lasting employment."

"That religion is best, which is incorporated with the actions and common traverses of our life ; and as there will be some foolish actions, so there will be matter for repentance : let this humble us, but not amaze or distract us."—*Ductor Dubitantium*, bk. i. chap. v. rule 5.

tation.  If she cannot be quite satisfied (as at times
I suppose she will not) with having broken through
her own rule in this instance, why cannot she add
one sentence to her Morning and Evening devotions,
relating to this particular subject ?  This, if made
habitual, would, as it seems to me, answer all purposes ; but she must not be fanciful, and imagine
one's prayers do no good if one is uncomfortable all
the time.  I am sure it would be bad enough with
some of us, if we let present comfort come into our
calculations on that matter.

    1827.

## LETTER XII.

To a Friend, newly Ordained ; Exhortations to
    Cheerfulness in Duties : Caution against over-
    strictness as to Recreations and Amusements.

    My dear ——,

    .... I am afraid .... that you are allowing sudden,
and (no doubt) substantially right, impressions on
the most important of all subjects to make you less
active, less cheerful, and less useful, than Providence
intended you to be.  Even in my narrow round of experience, I have seen so much that is really injurious
to truth and piety, arising from that view of the
Christian life which I understand you to incline to,
that I am truly grieved whenever I hear of any of
my friends taking it up.  I do not mean that it is

possible for a man to be too much in earnest about
religion, or to give up too much of his time to it:
on the contrary, he who takes the injunction "do all
to the glory of God," in the most literal sense, appears to me to come nearest to the true sense of it.
But then I differ from some whom I most sincerely
love and respect, in my interpretation of the maxim,
as applied to the present state of the world.  I do not
think the glory of God best promoted by a rigid
abstinence from amusements, except they be either
sinful in themselves, or carried to excess, or in some
other way ministering occasion to sin.  On the contrary, I believe that there is more charity lost, than
there is sobriety gained, by any unnecessary appearance of austerity.  Self-denial seems to mean, not
going out of the world, but walking warily and up-
rightly in it.  Nor can I well imagine any greater
service to society than is rendered by him, who
submits to its common routine, though something
wearisome, for this very reason : lest he should offend
his neighbours by unnecessary rigour.

Besides, if our neighbours' pleasures be harmless,
and we have it in our power to increase them, without breaking any law of God or man, is it quite
agreeable to the spirit of Christian Charity to refuse
to do so? Is it quite agreeable to such passages as
"Rejoice with them that do rejoice;" or to our
Saviour's example in working the miracle in Cana,
and in submitting to the reproach of being a man

gluttonous and a wine-bibber, rather than offend un-
thinking sinners by too much preciseness? Is it
quite agreeable to the general spirit of the Gospel?
which directs us, even when we fast, not to be of
a sad countenance, and which, next to inculcating
the necessity of a thorough inward change, seems
anxious to discourage any violent outward one, except when it is a plain duty.

On this head, my impression has been formed
a good deal, I believe, by the seventh chapter of the
first Epistle to the Corinthians, not from any direct
precepts, but from the general tone and tenor of its
morality. But whether it is the strength of my prejudice, I know not, but almost every time I look into
the New Testament, I feel the more convinced, that
the more quietly and calmly one sets about one's duty,
and the less one breaks through established customs,
always supposing them innocent in themselves, the
more nearly does one act according to the great
Exemplar there proposed.

You see I am giving you one proof, at least, that
I still consider you as an old friend : viz. lecturing
away at you, hastily. Very likely what I have said
may be not at all to your purpose : very likely it
may be a mistaken view which I have taken of the
matter, but I do assure you, it is a sincere and deliberate one ; not got up, as you may very naturally
have supposed, with a view to convince you. Indeed,
it is a point so continually occurring in practice,

that a man must have some principle of his own about it, and I am fully aware that no man can lay down his own rule for the standard of another's conduct. I hope, therefore, you will consider what I have written above as being simply the statement of my own rule, and some of the grounds on which it stands.

You yourself (or rather your reasoning part, whenever it can get the better of your feelings,) will be the best able to judge whether the rule suits your own situation and temperament, and whether the arguments are well founded or no. Only give me a line . . . . for indeed I am anxious to hear from you, and tell me how you are, and promise to give my sermon a candid consideration if it deserve it, and if not, to forgive me for having bothered you at all with it.

One thing more : I think I understood . . . . that your lowness of spirit arises in great measure from a fear that you have undertaken the priestly office without due preparation. Now without knowing more of the particulars than I do, it is impossible to say whether your fears are well grounded or not ; this, however, I will boldly say, that supposing them ever so just, it is not a life of inactive remorse or constant penance which is required of you, but one of all diligence and activity. I will put it in the words of one whose life I would recommend you to read with all speed, and who can never be suspected of making light of any miscarriage in so weighty an affair : it is Bishop Bull, in a sermon which probably you have read.    Speaking of the great danger of our calling, he says, " For mine own part, I cannot, I dare not justify myself, or plead not guilty before the Great Judge of Heaven and earth : but do upon the bended knees of my soul, bewail my sin, and implore His pardoning grace and mercy, crying mightily unto Him, Deliver me from this blood-guiltiness, O Lord."   But then he continues, " Having laid ourselves at God's feet, let us not lie idly there, but arise, and for the future do the work of God, with all faithfulness and industry."   I the rather recommend this excellent man to your study and imitation, because I think he has so completely refuted a notion, which I know several wise and good men entertain, of its being wrong to mingle literary pursuits, properly so called, with those of a Clergyman. The passage above is taken from the second volume of his English Works, lately republished, page 168 [d].

1817.

## LETTER XIII.

### To a Clergyman, on Amusements.

MY DEAR SIR,

Your communication is most deeply interesting : I only wish I may be able to speak truth and com-

[d] Vol. i. p. 164, Oxford, printed at the Clarendon Press.

fort for such a person as you describe. I feel very stupid : one can but try.

All my life long, I have been used to take what many would call the *laxer* view of common recreations and the ordinary pleasures of life, supposing them of course, innocent in themselves, and not so indulged as to give scandal, or withdraw the heart from God: and leaving it free to those who feel themselves inwardly called, and Providentially encouraged, to something higher—something like counsels of Perfection—to take their course.

The whole tenor of Holy Scripture, as expounded by the Church in all ages, and not least clearly by our own standard teachers, appears to me to bear out this view. Only think what a treasure of *secondary satisfactions* (so to call them) the Bible itself is: the perfection of poetry, language, and history,—its blessings on conjugal love, family delights, the ways of little children, the beauties and mysteries of art and nature. It seems to say, "Take all these and make much of them, for God's glory : be assured that there is nothing innocent so trifling, that it may not be thus sacrificed to Him." And when our Lord says, "Woe to them that laugh," &c., I understand Him to be warning us against a frivolous worldly temper, not against the moderate indulgence of the instinct which prompts laughter, to cheer those who need cheering ; or sometimes in a warning way, to correct those who need correcting. In all this, I believe

I concur with such writers as Hooker, Bp. Taylor, George Herbert, Isaac Walton, &c., not to mention foreign writers.

I should think the best and most blessed way for young persons under guidance, would be, to go upon these principles, watching themselves very carefully, and taking advice when needful, of course with earnest prayer on the special subject. If, then, Almighty God has some better thing for them than ordinary life, His Providence will guide them on to it : but the less they choose for themselves, the more humbly they await the indications of His will, the better.   I would point out that even in the life which is outwardly most secular there is room for the greatest Christianity in all parts of life.

These are but trite generalities, but they may suggest here and there a useful thought, and if you wished me to go more into detail I would gladly do so ; but it would be desirable to have more particulars ; personal knowledge would be most to the purpose if it could be had. . . .

Believe me with best wishes,<br>Very sincerely yours,

1860.                              J. KEBLE.

# LETTER XIV.

## To a Lady, on Spiritual Dryness.

MY DEAREST CHILD,

I have just been reading over your letter, and am more vexed than I can say, though not half so vexed as I ought to be, with myself, for not having answered it. I cannot say that engagements have hindered me. I might and ought to have written; neither am I quite so bad as to have forgotten you. It was the old bad habit. And now what can I say, more than you have heard and read in a much better form many times before? One thing I *will* say, for I am most firmly persuaded of it, that a great part of your dulness and dryness about holy things, probably the whole, so far as it is accountable for by human judgment, is a symptom of your illness: and I daresay you often feel the like distressing want of interest in other matters which you would fain take an interest in : I daresay you often have to rouse yourself up, and force yourself to be or seem amused with things which in former days would have taken hold of you without any effort. If it is so in ordinary things, then its not being so in religious services and meditations would be a merciful interference, more perhaps than one could reasonably expect ; and its not being granted, ought not to dishearten one, nor make one think oneself the

D

subject of a special judgment. Another thing is, that all religious meditation has a tendency, if it be not its direct work, to turn the mind's eye back as it were on itself; and this is necessarily a painful and wearisome effort, and causes a sort of aching which cannot well be endured when the frame or spirits are weakened by sickness of certain sorts: I suppose, then, that it is a provision of God's mercy to disqualify the mind in such cases for meditation, and keep it in a kind of dulness, which however uncomfortable, may be as good for the soul and mind, as sleepiness (which is often also most uncomfortable) is for the body. Any how it is, and must be, a grief to you, and so far part of His fatherly discipline : but if conscience, fairly examined, charges you with no more than you have by His Grace truly confessed and repented of (though *that* were ever such deadly sin,) you must not take this, any more than other troubles, as a token of wrath, but as an earnest (how strange soever it may seem to us) of great Love hereafter to be revealed ; pardoning Love, inexhaustible, everlasting Love. O my dear Child, only think of the joy and consolation, when all that is now crooked shall be made straight, and all that is wanting shall be numbered, and His forgiven ones shall see, once for all, how these distresses have served to purge them, perhaps, and make them white, and otherwise prepare them to see His Face with joy.

In the mean time I beg of you, do not be too
severe, do not strain your inward eye by turning it
too violently back upon itself: remember you are
bound for others' sake, as well as your own, to be,
if you can, and not only to seem, comfortable and
cheerful. Do not be afraid to take, as they come,
the little refreshments and amusements which His
mercy provides for you, and be not too nice in
comparing your interest in these with the dulness
you may possibly feel in direct religious exercises.
Take a lesson from your little ones (may He be
with them!) and be patient, or cheerfully thankful,
as the case may be, without blaming yourself for
what is in all probability God's visitation, no direct
fault of your own.

We have rather a cloud over us here at present,—
the loss of our dear kind —— and the public aspect
of Church matters. Our own households, I am thankful to say, are most thriving; and the Parish gets
dearer, and I seem to understand it better as the
time draws near for quitting it—I mean in the natural course of things : though what Lord John may
do to quicken it no one can say.

My dear love to —— and ——, and my wife's to
all, you especially.

Your very affec^te but not exemplary,
J. K.

# LETTER XV.

## To the Same.

MY VERY DEAR CHILD,

I have but one minute to say that your note was
a great comfort to me : although it did not at all
lessen the impression of my own woodenness, which
I carried away with me from our little conference.
I could at least have given a Priest's Benediction, and
that I now desire to do with all my heart and soul :
for you and all those who are now around you, and
whom at a distance you most think of. As for
advice, I can only say over and over what you know
far better than I : cast all your care upon Him,
both in respect of pain, and of regret for whatever, in your low state of health, may sometimes
appear doubtful to you in things past. Cast it all
upon Him.

Your loving and unworthy father in Him,

J. K.


# LETTER XVI.

## To a Young Lady, whose Father had forbidden her applying to him for Spiritual Advice.

MY DEAR YOUNG FRIEND,

I feel quite sure that by the blessing of God your
giving up what you had wished for, in the spirit

in which you try to do so, will be a far greater help to you than any special guidance in the world, much more that which you are now parting with. Indeed, I have a thought or two, but I will not trouble you with them, as to some of the probable reasons why things have been so ordered. But one great comfort is, it is a simple case, and there can be no doubt about the line of duty in it. . . .

With every kind wish to you and yours, and the best benediction that I can give, which I hope virtually to repeat every morning of my life,

I am always

Your affec^te friend,

J. KEBLE.

# LETTER XVII.

## To a Lady, on Observing Advent.

MY DEAR FRIEND AND CHILD, (it is well that you have one more real and better Father,) forgive me for not having written sooner—many things have interrupted me: and now I fear I must be more brief than I ought. . . .

The thought you speak of is, I suppose, not an unnatural one to occur to frail mortals, making in any sense an effort towards perfection. Whatever its origin be, it must be prayed against and not indulged : but I would not have you deal bitterly with yourself about it.   I suppose if a person go on gently following the leading of God's good Providence, and not pretending to take his lot into his own hands, he will not be suffered either rashly to undertake too much, or in frailty to swerve from what he has undertaken. . . .

For an Advent rule, I scarce know what to say: so incredibly ignorant and inexperienced am I, as you will find more and more.   But it occurs to me that perhaps during that season you might make the Wednesday another Friday, by some little hardness as your health and usefulness may bear, and by meditating for a stated time on the Four Last Things.

Ever, my dear child,
Your affec^{te},
J. KEBLE.

May I say that *I* very much need your remembrance just now ?

# LETTER XVIII.

## TO THE SAME, ON THE EXPECTED DEATH OF HER SISTER.

MY VERY DEAR CHILD,

I need not say, Be of good comfort, HE says it so plainly.   And among other things which occur as very comforting, and which will, I doubt not, come out more and more when it is thought all over, like stars in the sky, it seems so good that your dear Sister was allowed those quiet months at ——, where she was probably able to adorn herself for this time, more tranquilly than she could well have done elsewhere.

We shall try and pray for her as you desire : no harm to do so, if she should have gone into another room.

Y<sup>r</sup> most affec<sup>te</sup>,

J. K.

## LETTER XIX.

### ON THE EVILS RESULTING FROM DISUSE OF CONFESSION IN THE ENGLISH CHURCH.

ANOTHER reason for my being a worse correspondent than usual, is that somehow or another the Parish takes up more and more time ; as one gets more acquainted with the people, more and more things occur which make me think a visit worth while. This is a reason for which I ought to be very thankful, though it is sad to think, after all, how very little one knows of one's people. We go on working in the dark, and in the dark it will be, until the rule of systematic Confession is revived in our Church.

This is one of the things which make persons like Mr. Gladstone, however competent in most respects, yet on the whole incompetent judges of the real working of our English system. They do not, they cannot, unless they were tried as we are, form an adequate notion, how absolutely we are in our parishes like people whose lantern has blown out, and who are feeling their way, and continually stepping in puddles and splotches of mud, which they think are dry stones.

Then the tradition which goes by the name of Justification by Faith, and which in reality means that one who has sinned, and is sorry for it, is as if he had not sinned, blights and benumbs one in every limb, in trying to make people aware of their real state.

These are the sort of things, and not the want of handsome Churches, and respect for Church Authority, and such like comparatively external points, which make me at times feel so disheartened about our system altogether, and cause a suspicion, against one's will, that the life is gone or going out of it.

And this is why I so deprecate the word and the idea of Protestantism, because it seems inseparable to me from "Every man his own absolver;" that is, in other words, the same as "Peace where there is no peace," and mere shadows of Repentance.

# LETTER XX.

### TO ONE HINDERED FROM CONFESSION FOR A TIME, BY HER STATE OF HEALTH.

MY VERY DEAR DAUGHTER (tho' it seems to me almost presumptuous to call you so), I send you my Blessing with all my heart : you have it every morning : but by all means do as you are bid in keeping as quiet as possible just now.

I shall be at your command when —— thinks well, and not before : and it is a great mercy that you are preserved from scruples and distressing thoughts, so that you can peacefully acquiesce in what you are told is best. In fact what can we desire better, than that He should take us entirely into His own Hands; which seems to be His way of dealing with your father's house. . . . . And so with all good Advent wishes I rest (in Him whom we would serve),

Your loving but not very worthy<br>Father & Friend,<br>J. K.

# LETTER XXI.

## To a Clergyman, on the Choice of a Curate.

My dear ——,

I wish I could help you to a good Curate, but you are one out of three very pressing applications which I received about the same time. I fear there will be more and more difficulty in getting such helpers as we should thoroughly like, as the effect of what the Bishops and Heads of Houses have been doing for the last three years comes to be more felt. Numbers of young men, such as one should most wish to have, are, I imagine, deterred from ordination, by fearing that they should be more or less mixed up with the Protestant interpretation of the Articles. . . .

Perhaps it is hardly worth mentioning to you, but I see the name of a Mr. ——, mentioned as having been dismissed from a London Cure by the Bishop, for preaching a sermon on Confession. I think if I wanted a Curate, I should enquire about him, not of course make him an offer at once, but try to ascertain through others whether he was a good and discreet man, and if he were, give him a preference. Whoever can discreetly and effectually bring in Confession, will do, I should think, one of the best things for this poor Church as she is at present.

## LETTER XXII.

### ON CONFESSION AND FASTING.

MY DEAR FRIEND,

I really do not know of any particular in which at present I can amend your suggestions. For my own case (for miserable recollections make me shrink from hearing confessions), I could wish that you had chosen some other for *that* part of your course; but I would not on any account check you, if you think it good for yourself. I have not a copy of the devotions which have been adopted, and if I had, I do not know that I should like to be forward in suggesting alterations in devotional forms actually adopted. There seems a risk of disturbing people.

I hope you will be careful about the Fasting, and keep a *medical conscience* in your own bosom or that of some friend who may be trusted. Family men (I mean those who live with others) are embarrassed sometimes by the effect of their example on those others, to whom perhaps what *they* do may be imprudent. Such cases I suppose are provided for by the rule of "Mercy not Sacrifice," until the too tender conscience of the other party can be sufficiently hardened.

## LETTER XXIII.

### To a Father, on the Death of his Child.

WHAT can such an one as I am say to comfort
a Father at such a time as this must be to you
that you do not know much better yourself? but
in all grief it is something to see in a friend's hand-
writing that he is trying at least to sympathize
with one, and of this you may be sure on my part.
And whilst we are writing, and thinking, and trying,
we are all, if we are not wanting to ourselves, coming
nearer the perfect Comfort, of which all these are
but shadows.  How remarkable that so soon after
——'s affliction, you should be visited in the same
way.  Who knows how far your thoughts of him,.
or other circumstances connected with his loss, may
have prepared you and yours for this blow? or how
the rest and happiness of the one departed may be
entwined with that of the other?  There is nothing
wrong, I trust, in dwelling upon such thoughts when
they come into one's mind ; and if they help to make
one muse on sudden trials with resignation and awe,
may we not think they were intended, and are approved of? . . . .

Surely, as you have always been helped to feel
for others, so many and many both here and There
will be helped to feel and pray for you : and now
we have the comfort of knowing, what we were even

afraid to dream of until Providence recalled our thoughts, as of late, to the Ancient Church, that we may innocently and piously pray for our departed, and that they no doubt remember and pray for us. Surely that one thing is worth a great deal of trouble and annoyance, such as seems from day to day to be gathering like a cloud around us.

Surely, too, it is something to know that dear children are safe from the manifold and most bewildering trials which seem fast coming upon us. Happy those who have not to charge themselves with some part of the public evil, on account either of their meddling with things too high for them, or touching God's pure truth when themselves impure. This is, by-the-bye, to bespeak your remembrance, now when affliction has brought you, in a manner, unusually near the Throne.

## LETTER XXIV.

### ON SPEAKING FREELY OF THE DEPARTED.

I NEED not say to you, because you must know it full well, how desirable it is to lose no time in using ourselves to speak freely and calmly to one another of those who are out of sight, as though they were, as they are, *only* out of sight.

## LETTER XXV.

### ON THE SAME.

MAY it please Him that when the few years are over during which we shall be in different rooms in God's House, one may not be found quite unworthy to meet him again. And surely one may hope this, since to those who are forgiven it will be permitted to see even His Face, Who made —— and all His saints what they are . . .

I do hope that you will, as soon as you can, use yourself to name his name, and speak freely of him at home and among friends. I fear it may be doing violence to yourself at first; but I dread your shrinking from the subject too much. It will be such a loss of comfort to yourself and others : and one feels so sure of what he would wish.

## LETTER XXVI.

### ON PRAYER FOR THE DEPARTED.

I CANNOT doubt that He who is the true Comforter has been and will be with you, tempering your loneliness with sweet thoughts, such as He only can impart, and that all that happens about your work and your dear children especially, will be providentially ordered to help and soothe you.

For one thing, I will venture to send you a sort of suffrage, I believe from Bishop Andrewes, which one very unworthy person at least has used for years. with far greater comfort than he deserves.

. "Remember Thy servants and handmaidens which have departed hence in the Lord, especially —— and all others to whom our remembrance is due; give them eternal rest and peace in Thy Heavenly Kingdom, and to us such a measure of Communion with them, as Thou knowest to be best for us. And bring us all to serve Thee in Thine eternal Kingdom when Thou wilt, and as Thou wilt, only without shame or sin. Forgive my presumption and accept my prayers, as Thou didst the prayers of Thine ancient Church, through Jesus Christ our Lord."

We think a great deal of you, my very dear friends, though some of us not half enough; but no doubt you are thought of there, where thoughts are deeds, and deeds are blessings for ever. You must not be too much disheartened, nor blame yourselves, if now at your first coming home, you do not feel so much alive as you would wish to the many blessings which are still spared even to your sight: it is a natural yearning which He who spared not His own Body, nor His Mother's grief, will turn into a great grace for you all.

## LETTER XXVII.

### ADVICE CONCERNING CONFESSION.

MY DEAR ——,

. . . . Two points in your statement (to me very full of reproach) make your case, as it seems to me, a comparatively simple one : the first, that you were without early religious instruction ; the other, that you did not relapse after Communion. This being so, and our Church not laying down any rule how *particular* a confession should be, I think the degree of detail may best be left to your own judgment, according as you may seem to want guidance in any point, or as the act of confessing may relieve your own mind as a penitential exercise.

The Absolution appears in this case so distinctly sealed beforehand by the Judge Himself, that I should not think of *requiring* more than the naming of the crimes and bad habits for which it was desired. And I should not doubt that you might by God's blessing cheerfully go to His Altar, as usual with you. Even in the Roman Church, I believe, provision is made for the case of a penitent fully intending to confess, and only waiting till he has opportunity. Of course I may be mistaken, . . . . but thus it appears to me. Would it not be well to consult some other person ? though I shall be most thankful, if it please God to make me of any use or comfort to you.

Ever believe me, dear ——,

Very sincerely yours,

J. KEBLE.

## LETTER XXVIII.

TO AN OFFICER IN THE ARMY, ON CONVERSATION
AT MESS, &c.

MY DEAR FRIEND,

Forgive my delay in writing. I have really been a little perplexed what to say about your case of the dinner and unpleasant conversation. It seems to me one in which a very great deal must depend on the chance of doing good at some future time, by bearing with undesirable things for a while. In the natural course of things you will be acquiring rank before very long, and this will enable you perhaps to give a permanent check to what is disagreeable, and, for the sake of this, it may be your duty to go on. It must be very unpleasant, for it must be in fact a series of cases of conscience continually occurring; instances, I mean, which cause you to doubt whether you should be silent, or testify, or quit the company. One's mind must, I suppose, be made up upon consideration of the general effect and tendency of what takes place both upon oneself and others. Things

E

may be bad, yet one may have good reason for
thinking that they would be worse if one went away.
I suppose it is open to you to make excuses from
time to time, and so get rid of a good many of the
Friday · dinners ; and, in the meantime, since by
God's blessing you are tolerably sure of your purpose, you can best judge for yourself upon comparing particulars, and choose the least of two
evils.

About self-examination and meditation I have just
the same difficulty that you speak of. . . . . But I
should suppose that a few sentences of (e.g.) the
Decades in Taylor's "Golden Grove," or out of Bp.
Wilson's "Maxims," or such poems as Bp. Ken's Morning Hymn, or (best of all) the Gospel History, or our
Lord's discourses, resolutely thought on for a few
minutes, with real persevering endeavour to exclude
other thoughts, might by degrees answer the purpose
in some measure, and train a person to think (if one
may say so) for himself. The self-examination is
comparatively easy when a person is pretty well
aware of his own feelings ; but of course, the best
can perform it but imperfectly ; and beginners must
not be disheartened if they seem to themselves to do
little or nothing.

I must say good night, for it is getting very late,
and write again if anything more occurs. It is indeed
a great comfort to know of one's being remembered
and thought of regularly, by a friendly heart, in one's

great need, and I hope we shall be able to go on quietly with that observance. . . . .

Church and academical matters look, I fear, very ominous, and there is much need that every one should pray for this Church and for all who are perplexed in it.

Ever y<sup>r</sup> very affec<sup>te</sup>,<br>J. KEBLE.

## LETTER XXIX.

### To the Same, sending a Form of Penitential Prayer.

My dear Friend,

I have been on the point of addressing you several times, and hardly know what has hindered me, except, for one thing, that I have not been able to fix upon any collect which seemed as if it would quite suit our purpose, which, however, I have not lost sight of, as I trust you have not. I like your notion of the 51st Psalm, with a short collect, very much, and have tried to act upon it, but have hitherto found none in our P. Book which suited exactly. That for Ash-Wednesday seemed to do best. But to-day I have been turning over the Roman Missal, and one has occurred, which, with a very slight turn in the translation, seems eligible. I will write it at the foot of this. For the time, I am such a sort of person that I cannot depend on myself to be punctual; only

I should say that in general sometime between 2 and 4 o'clock I shall hope to say this Service, and shall think of you doing the same; unless you wish for any alteration. Provided we substantially remember each other, I am indifferent about the details.... With all kind regards, believe me affectionately, though most undeservingly, yours,

J. KEBLE.

### PROPOSED SERVICE.

Lord have mercy, &c.

Our Father.

℣. Turn us, O God our Saviour:

℟. And let Thine anger cease from us.

*Antiphon.* Wash me throughly from my wickedness, and cleanse me from my sin.

Psalm 51.

*Antiphon*, as before.

Let us pray.

O God, Who towards all that trust in Thee delightest in pity rather than in anger, grant unto us worthily to bewail (and do meet penance for) the evils which we have done: that we may obtain the grace of Thy consolation: through our Lord Jesus Christ.

The Lord bless us, &c. (as at the end of the Commination Service.)

# LETTER XXX.

To the Same, on United Prayer for the Church.

My dear Friend,

. . . . . . I have been desiring R. to think of some regular prayer for the Church of England, and perplexed spirits within her pale, to be used at one of the hours.  P. is very desirous of it, and so are many others.  What he thought of was the Lord's Prayer with that special intention, and the 130th Psalm.  Each might use it at his own hour, but the point would be, to have it at *some* time in the twenty-four hours.  So of your prayer for Church extension : your way is a very good one, and I should be sorry to interfere with it.  Another, perhaps, might prefer the Lord's Prayer with *that* intention, and the 67th or some such Psalm.  The great point is to know that people are praying *for the same thing, daily.*

I am very glad of S. Augustine's College, and of Medley's appointment, and of what I hear of Ceylon.  Really, at present, the colonial Churches appear the most encouraging part of our Church, and I cannot but take courage when I think of them.  What a comfort it must be to the Bishop of London.  What follows refers to your former letter.  With regard to ——, I will only say two things,—that I could wish him to be particularly remembered in the Intercession mentioned above, and that all I come to see and know of him makes me think more highly of him.

My own feeling about the Churches is, that England, Rome, and Greece, being all, I trust and hope, parts of the one Church, no person ought to leave that one of the three in which God's Providence has placed him, nor yet to feel jealous or hostile towards the others, but rather as our Lord spoke of the man who was casting out devils in His Name, but not following with the Apostles. Whether this view would be tenable, if I had more learning and acuteness, I cannot say. In the meantime, I feel sure that unlearned Englishmen cannot be very wrong if they go in all points by the Prayer-book. . . . .

Y<sup>n</sup> affec<sup>tly</sup>,

J. KEBLE.

## LETTER XXXI.

To the Same, on Private Eucharistical Prayer.

My dear ——,

I am sorry that I should be again a defaulter, the rather as I was actually consoling myself with the thought that this time you were in my debt, and even now I cannot realize my having heard from you since I wrote, but I have no doubt that you are right ; and now I think of it again, it does strike me that I don't remember ever thanking you for your kind information about the non-rejection of the Communion Office at Trinity College, and yet few things that I have heard of lately have given me so much pleasure. For *us*, I think it may be even better than as if that Office had been exclusively adopted; it brings before men so clearly the fact that the two offices are reconcileable, and that this can only be by adopting the higher interpretation of ours.

Now with regard to your question. I see no objection whatever to a private layman's using in his Eucharistical devotions any such portion of an old orthodox Liturgy as that which you have sent to me. Besides Bishop Wilson, we have in the "Holy Living," and Bp. Andrewes, long extracts from various Liturgies, proposed as part of private devotion, and surely there is a special consolation in using what comes recommended by the Ancient Church. I use, or try to use, something of the kind, very like your extract from S. James's Liturgy. I am not aware of any objection to a person's privately using the word "offer" as you do. In Thomas à Kempis (to mention no more) there is, if I mistake not, ample precedent for it.

I apprehend we may, without fault, mention in our commemoration of the dead any who had departed, being not expressly out of communion with the Church. . . . . With our kindest regards,

Your affec<sup>te</sup>,

J. KEBLE.

## LETTER XXXII.

### To a Lady, an entire Stranger, on Repentance.

My dear Madam,

Pray forgive my delay : I have been unusually busy
in the Parish, and now have only time to write a
short, and, I fear, unsatisfactory letter.  But I hope
you will believe that I sincerely sympathize with
your distress, and shall be only too glad if I may
be the means of helping you at all.

Your question, "What is Repentance?" may be
answered by referring you to almost any of the devotional Books generally received either among English or Roman Catholics ; the regular account of it
being, that it includes Contrition, Confession, and
Satisfaction,—but I rather suppose that all this is
familiar to you, and that you are rather anxious for
some way of testing your own feelings and doings,
than for rules and definitions concerning Repentance
in general.  Among English Books I do not, at this
moment, recollect a better help than Kettlewell's
"Companion to the Penitent ;" and many persons
have found, I believe, exceeding benefit by the use
of the Third Part of " The Paradise of the Christian
Soul, translated and adapted to the use of the English Church." I will not at present mention more
Books than these ; but I am very anxious that you
should be quite aware of one thing, which both these

and (I apprehend) all other Books which treat truly of the subject, are careful to inculcate, viz. that the *wish*, the *continued wish* to be contrite, *is* contrition: the *wish* to hate one's evil self *is* the beginning of such hatred. A person who feels it in the slightest degree, and encourages the feeling, and tries to have more of it, and is grieved not to have more,—such an one, so far, is surely coming to our Lord, and "him that is coming unto Him, He will in no wise cast out." Undoubtedly the first effort at all this will be very faint and imperfect, but so are all our beginnings, and our *perceiving them* to be such is a good sign, not a bad one. The only sure and sufficient test of reality in one's feelings, I suppose to be our *conduct*, i.e. our deliberate thoughts, our words, and our actions, and especially in little every-day unnoticed and unnoticeable matters: if we are gradually trying more and more to bring them into captivity to the love of God and our neighbour, we may have the comfortable hope that God accepts our Repentance, however imperfect. In your own case, if I understand your letter rightly, submission to a great degree of spiritual loneliness seems a main part of the trial. If you can submit to doubt, per-plexity, misgivings, even to desolation, as to bereave-ment or bodily pain, striving to make the best of it, and take it cheerfully as part of His gracious deal-ings with you, and putting down every complaining thought either of your personal or ecclesiastical posi-

tion, I trust that in His good time you will find that
you are in a sure and safe way.

: Your question about dancing, &c., is of a kind
which, I believe, the best advisers are used to answer
conditionally. Such things, they say, are not bad
in themselves, but in the abuse of them ; and I suppose it very often happens that persons, if they use
them at all, find them so instrumental to one bad
feeling or another, that their wisest course, if they
can choose, is to refrain from them. But I can conceive cases where it would be unloving, or undutiful,
to act strictly in this rule ; where, for example, the
wish of parents is concerned. I can even conceive
cases where it would be more real self-denial to go
to such a party than to stay away from it. One can
scarcely lay down a universal rule ; it must depend
on one's own inward temptations, and on the degree
of scandal likely to be given to others.

Pray make use of me, such as I am, without scruple,
if I can be of the smallest comfort to you. Should
anything further occur to me, I will write without
waiting to hear from you again. With earnest
wishes for your comfort and best welfare, I am,
dear Madam,

Very faithfully yours,

J. K.

# LETTER XXXIII.

To the Same. — Meaning of Satisfaction. — Safe Rule in Church Difficulties.—On Feelings and Conduct.

My dear ——,

..... To take the topics of your letter in order. The word "satisfaction" is used by Divines—Hooker for example—to express those good works, words, and thoughts, by which a contrite heart would naturally express its desire to make amends, if it could, for the wrong done, not only to our brethren, but also to our God and Saviour, by our sins : worthy fruits of Penance the Commination Service calls them ; and although, of course, there can be no merit in them, strictly speaking, yet it has always been considered in the Church that He graciously accepts and rewards them : the penitential fasts, sackcloth, &c., of the Old Testament, and the "revenge" spoken of in the New (2 Cor. vii. 11), are, I suppose, cases in point.

Well may we grieve and humble ourselves for the state of our Church ; but, at the same time, we should do well to consider always how great a favour it is that we have a Church at all, that we are not like North Africa, or Asia Minor, almost or quite cut off for our sins ; and with all our might let us pray against any such grief as throws off the blame of

what is wrong from ourselves, on our condition, i.e.
on God's Providence. I only wish that I and all
who are tempted by such feelings, may be guided
to suppress them, until such time as we have made
*thorough* trial of our Prayer-books, according to our
means. I am greatly mistaken if that simple rule
would not prove, in God's good time, sooner or later,
a way of Peace and Truth, to every one who tries it
in earnest. But we must make up our minds to any
degree of doubt and misgiving that may be ordained
to punish and try us. In our days, when there is
comparatively no persecution, who knows but these
inward struggles may be the appointed way of per-
fecting those whom He favours.

To the question regarding conduct and feeling,
I should say, without any doubt or hesitation at
all, that the approbation of Him who sees in secret
depends not on conscious emotions, but on sincere
endeavours to obey Him. "This is the love of God,
that we keep His commandments." Do so because
it is your duty, and put your heart in His Hands
by Prayer, and He will deal with it as He knows
best ; by-and-by you will find that you have been
loving Him, perhaps even when you felt coldest.
Our conduct He leaves to ourselves, but our feelings
He keeps, in great measure, in His own Hands. You
wish to feel love, and you know that "if there be
first a willing mind, it is accepted according to that
a man hath, and not according to that he hath not."

Only beware of unduly loving any creature, and that is just what our conduct, well watched, will test. I suppose it much safer for most of us to be distressed with the fear that we do not love God, than to be pleasing ourselves with the thought that we do love Him. It must require a very high tone of conduct to be safe in thinking that we enter consciously into the spirit of such a book as the "Imitation of Christ."

With regard to the very painful subject with which your letter concludes, I have been used to think, that we are in no sort judges how far "invincible ignorance" may excuse a person in the sight of God for any degree of speculative unbelief, *provided he really tries to act up to the light vouchsafed.* This way of thinking the Fathers of old applied to the cases of the good and virtuous heathens, and, by parity of reasoning, it may, one should think, apply to many cases among ourselves, whom the letter of our formularies would seem to condemn. Why, then, may you not hope humbly, that at some time, in some state or other, the true faith and the mercy which it reveals may, in some degree at least, reach to such an amiable person as you describe, though we may not see or know how? In the meantime, your speaking or not on such matters, is surely a question of expediency, depending on the chance of doing good. You can but watch and pray for opportunity and guidance, and help to make the most of any opening that may be granted. Sayings, doings, and looks, which seem very slight in themselves, have often a good deal of virtue, I believe, in such cases; and waiting on sickness or decline, gives occasion sometimes to unexpected ways of helping those whom we love.

Circumstances separated me a good deal from my dear friend R. H. Froude (of whom you ask), in his last illness; but I have heard enough of it to say with some confidence, that he did enjoy that comfortable hope which the Gospel offers to sincere penitents, both for a good while before, and also especially on his death-bed.

I seem to have written very coldly on many most touching subjects; but if, by His undeserved mercy, I have been able to suggest anything which may help or comfort you, it will be a real joy to me: and I beg of you, my dear young Lady, to have no scruple in writing as often and as much as may seem to relieve you or do you good. I fear you will often find my answers very unsatisfactory: if you wished it, I could introduce you to the correspondence of others far more likely to help you than I am. In any case, believe me, with all best wishes,

Your affectionate Friend and Servant in our Lord
JOHN KEBLE.

# LETTER XXXIV.

### To the Same, on Catholic Yearnings. Cheering Hopes for the Church of England.

My dear ——,

I will no longer delay acknowledging your last letter, which was indeed a great comfort to me, as giving me reason to hope I might be of some little use to you, which is more than I am fit to dare hope for. But I am too busy or too lazy to answer it as it ought to be answered. You must just take what occurs to me on its topics in their order. I can quite enter into the forlorn feeling of being alone in your Catholic yearnings: but, in the first place, no doubt there are many even in —— who sympathise with you, if you could but know them : and, in the next place, it is one of the privileges (which are also the trials) of a Catholic mind, to depend very much on distant unseen sympathies—to be "never less alone, than when alone." S. Paul in his imprisonment seems to have had a great deal of this feeling, and a person in your circumstances may surely without presumption welcome any thoughts of the kind, provided they encourage no dreamy neglect of present duties. You ask if I have hope of our Church. Yes, indeed, by the blessing of God, I have a very comfortable and *growing* hope, that a better generation is coming on. I seem to see such an improvement

in the younger clergy, and, indeed, among the young
people of the higher orders generally.   People seem
to me to think rather more of their Baptism than
they did : though the contrary notion, which you
(I think justly) call Heresy, has been of course called
out and rendered rampant by the very opposition as
well as by other things. . . .

Pray do not *ever* feel the least scruple in writing
to me, if it is any comfort or use to you.   I cannot
say to you what a help it is to me, when such hints
as I can give seem to do good instead of harm.
I hope to be remembered in your Prayers at this
blessed season, and to remember you also.   Hitherto
I have done so, I believe, daily since your first letter.
May He who was this day made man, be your Guide
and your Comforter by His good Spirit.   Believe
me always

Very truly and aff<sup>ly</sup> yours,<br>J. KEBLE.

## LETTER XXXV.

To the Same, on Meditation, Fasting, and sensible
Comfort in Devotion.

My dear ——,

Do not think that I had forgotten you : your circumstances are far too interesting for that : I believe
I try every Morning to remember your name in my
prayers, such as they are.

For Meditation on the Passion of our Lord, I should think Mr. Isaac Williams' two portions of a Harmony of the Gospels, with a sort of Commentary, entitled, the Holy Week, and the Passion, would be found very useful. Bishop Taylor, in his " Life of Christ," will suggest a good deal. There are also two little publications, which might help : " The Cross of Christ," edited by Dr. Hook ; and " Short Meditations and Prayers on the Passion," published by Longman, and printed at Lymington. If I add those of Bp. Andrewes' Sermons which relate to the Passion, I shall at least have specified an abundant store of matter for meditation : but I suppose a few Books of the kind, well studied, are commonly more profitable than many.

Of Fasting, I think Divines commonly say, that it has three distinct ends : 1. Mortification, that is, assisting to overcome the natural man, and rendering us more able to resist temptation, such as S. Paul speaks of, 1 Cor. ix. ; 2ndly, Penance, i.e. helping and expressing contrition for sins past, as when the same S. Paul, on his conversion, fasted three days; and 3rdly, Contemplation, assisting the mind to withdraw itself from earthly things, of which Moses' fast is commonly considered an instance. You will find some useful remarks on this matter in Bp. Taylor's " Holy Living," and in the Fifth Book of Hooker's " Ecclesiastical Polity."

I have kept back to the last the most delicate and

F

difficult of your inquiries,—difficult to me, not so much
from any doubt I have as to the substance of the
Truth, as from a fear that I shall not be able to
speak of it as I ought, to a tender spirit, such as I
conceive yours to be. The truth, as I take it, is that
spiritual ease and comfort is so far like that of the
body, that, while we all naturally long for it, our
Great Father knows it not to be good for us all, and
so He denies it to some, and grants it to others, in
ways and degrees, the rule of which is secret to us.
To say that our *sensible* comfort and assurance is
a sure or necessary sign of God's favour, *must* be
a mistake, if it were only that it contradicts our
Lord's agony, and the feeling that He had on the
Cross, not to speak of many saintly examples in
Scripture : and to say, that no one of " your way of
thinking" is made (humanly speaking) happy thereby,
contradicts, I should say, one's daily and hourly experience. I thank God I could mention very many,
who are (to all human appearance) plain instances to
the contrary of such a saying. At any rate, I cannot
but think, that the whole of Scripture from beginning to end, could we read it with an unbiassed eye,
would quite disenchant us, if I may so say, of the
notion of assurance and comfort being the measure
of spiritual perfection. Perhaps no other Book could
be mentioned, after the Bible, more likely to quiet
a person's mind with the true impression on this subject, than Thomas à Kempis on the " Imitation of

Christ," which has been translated . . . . so as to make
it very suitable for English readers. There are also
two Sermons of Hooker's, one on the Perpetuity of
Faith in the Elect, the other called a Remedy for
Sorrow and Fear ; and there is Bp. Wilson's "Sacra
Privata," which contains a great treasure of devotional thought on this very subject. For my own
part, I should be quite miserable if I thought, as your
friends appear to think, that the present comfort and
satisfaction of a person's mind is in any degree a test
and measure of his being in favour of God. If it were
so, how could it be said, that the Peace of God
"passeth all understanding ?" or (as Luther, I believe,
expressed it), that many have it not, who make sure
of it ; some, who seem almost to despair of it, truly
have it ? Surely it is too high and blessed a gift to
be tested and analysed by any emotions, or by any
reasoning of ours. The holy writers seem rather to
speak of it as of a kind of instinct, like infants' trust
in their mothers, than as of a definite feeling or view,
which we can experience or reflect upon. I should
say to you, then, my dear young friend, thank God
and take courage, trusting entirely to His goodness,
who has enabled, and will still further enable, you to
contend with some degree of success against your
daily defects and infirmities. One of these overcome
by His aid, is worth whole years of supposed security
and highly-wrought feeling, without such earnest self-
mastery. I shall be very anxious to hear from you

again on this matter, when you have time and incli-
nation to favour me with a line.  Meanwhile, believe me,

Yours faithfully in Him,

J. KEBLE.

## LETTER XXXVI.

### To the Same, on Contrition.

My dear ——,

.... I will now recur to the principal topic of your
letter, so far as to say, that I believe all the Masters
of devotion are agreed, that the wish to be contrite,
continued and carefully encouraged, is in God's sight
not only the beginning of contrition, but the very
exercise of the habit itself, implying, as it does, habitual watchfulness and great jealousy of oneself in
regard of whatever indulgences and employments
are found to lessen tenderness of conscience, and the
sense that one ought to be penitent.  In short, I
should say that the letter which I have now before
me, in which the writer deplores her want of contrition, is in itself an outpouring of a truly contrite
heart, and as such I trust and believe has been graciously accepted, with many other like thoughts and
words, by Him, who can and will make the least that
we try to do worthy of Him : and that He has
blessed, and will bless you, with many a holy and

fruitful Communion, in token of His acceptance of
the feelings which you are ashamed of, but which
He has long ago declared Himself pleased with,
even when He said to Mary of Bethany, "She hath
done what she could." Your sense of His mercy in
preserving you from grievous sin and giving you an
early sense of His goodness, is far indeed from being
any blemish in such contrition as I am speaking of:
and as to the bitterness of feeling which holy men
often express, I can only say, what I have said to
you before, that feelings are not directly in our own
power, any more than tears are. The will and the
wish, in this as in other things, are, I doubt not,
a true sacrifice of God.

Did you ever happen to read the Life of James
Bonnell, or the Journal of the late Mrs. Trimmer, or
a book published a few years since, called "Memorials of a departed Friend?" They all of them might
be thought by some deficient in contrition, yet who
can doubt that the writers were truly contrite and
humble persons?

My dear young Friend, I am not, I verily believe,
in any degree flattering you, but only delivering what
I am persuaded is His message, when I bid you again
to "thank God and take courage," and to go cheerfully on in the same way, wherein He has mercifully
led you so far: the more lonely, the more sure, in
one sense, of His special aid.

Once more forgive me, and if you can, give me

something to do or write for you, that I may in some sort make up for this very unkind neglect.

And believe me,

In Him whom we would serve,

Your sincere Friend,

J. KEBLE.

## LETTER XXXVII.

To a Clergyman, on admitting to Communion one Burdened in Conscience, who had not made formal Confession.

I THINK, on referring to the letters I have received from the person you allude to, that you a little mis-apprehend the facts of the case, in this respect, that what I have received is neither a confession, nor does it express any urgent or settled longing for confes-sion, as the necessary and ordained means for remis-sion of sins. Rather it speaks primarily of need of guidance, and of confession only, or chiefly, so far as preliminary to such guidance. And so far is it from being of the nature of a confession properly so called, that it would not enable me to judge posi-tively whether you are correct or no in your notion of the seriousness of the case. What I did, therefore, was simply this, (so far as I feel at liberty to speak of it.) A person in doubt and anxiety applies to me, not knowing for certain whether she should confess to me or not, but willing to do so, if it were thought right, when opportunity should be given, and wishing for some hints how to go on in the meantime. I send her some such hints which I happen to have by me, not directing her to act by them, but for the chance of their suiting her, and amongst them is one recommendation of frequent Communion.

You see, therefore, it is not (so far as I can say) quite the case which you put; I am not quite sure that there is deadly sin upon the conscience, nor yet that the person looks to Confession as the one way in which the sin may be remitted. So far as I know, you might perhaps admit her to Communion, without infringing your own rule. But it is very likely that on both these points you know more than I do as yet.

I shall, of course, advise the person not to present herself for Holy Communion in your church without your express permission. But what if she should ask me, " May I receive elsewhere ?"

I am, (to my shame,) for many reasons, a very inadequate judge of such matters, with very little either of reading or experience. But I have no doubt that *if* we are bound in this matter by the rules of the Roman Catholic Church, the law is as you lay it down, only I thought it had been more stringent. I thought the Roman Catholic Church had said, "No man with deadly sin upon his conscience must communicate without special private Absolution," without reference to the opinion or desire of the individual : whereas you, if I rightly understand you, would admit a person who was satisfied in conscience, without any thought of priestly absolution. But the moment *that* is wished for, you consider the person under a different rule. You think that then all the strict requirements of the foreign confessional take place. Now this is what I have not yet been able to understand. I should have thought that if the Priest and Penitent between them may decide in each case on that greatest point, whether there shall be Auricular Confession or no, much more is it left to them to judge on the details connected with it : e.g. how minute it should be ; whether read or merely spoken, &c. ; and, amongst other things, how it should be timed, and whether or no the delay of it should keep a person from the Holy Communion. One sees, of course, that there is the greatest room for abuse and self-deceit in these things, as there is, no doubt, in the permission to dispense with Auricular Confession altogether, which yet I believe you allow to be granted by our Church. We may wish it otherwise, but we must take things as we find them ; and although it would greatly simplify matters, and make one's task, in a certain sense, much easier, to tie ourselves to the foreign rules, I feel that, in spite of ourselves, the line which our Church has taken compels us to modify them in very charity to the many souls which would, I fear, otherwise be repelled from their best hope of recovery.

After all, I do not know that in the particular case there is so much difference between us. It may be reduced, I think, to this, that you would repel from Holy Communion any one who was but longing for Auricular Confession from an indefinite notion that it might do him good in the way of deliverance from grievous sin : *I* should say, " You ought not to come till you have so confessed, if you *distinctly* believe this to be the one way of deliverance." And I can easily conceive that in most cases I might *recommend* yours as the safest way, though I do not see that our Church authorizes me to *insist* on it in *all* cases.

I think I ought to apologize for interfering, as I seem to have done, with your flock ; and yet I hardly know how I can help it. I trust and hope that all will end well.

I shall recommend the person, if in doubt, to abstain as you direct, and take it as a penance ; if free in conscience, and the burthen of abstinence very unsettling, I might perhaps yield to her communicating elsewhere at Easter.

## LETTER XXXVIII.

### To a Clergyman, on dealing with one under Special Temptation.

I do not see how you could give better advice than you have done, in the distressing, but by no means uncommon, case which you have partly described

to me.  I fancy that I quite understand it, as far as
I can understand other people's cases ; and that it is,
in all probability, partly a trial permitted by the
Almighty in the way of bodily and nervous disease,
partly an effort of the Evil One to divert the soul
from those regular religious exercises, which he knows
are its appointed means of health and security.  The
sceptical feelings you mention, point strongly that
way.  I cannot consider him responsible either for
them, or for his devotional distractions.  He confesses
them, prays against them, hates them in his heart,
wishes to have more poignant anguish for them, gives
them no manner of encouragement : how, then, can
they be accounted his, and not his enemy's ?

I should have most comfortable and sure hope that,
by steadily persisting in such a course as you describe, he will turn these distresses into occasions of
blessing, whether he feels it so in this world, or no.
Does he know the " Spiritual Combat," and Thomas
à Kempis ? there is much in both of them to his
purpose . . . . I would warn your friend especially
against late hours, and loss of sleep.  Any other sort
of asceticism would be better than that.

# LETTER XXXIX.

### To a young Layman, on Notes of the Church : Advice as to Books and Conversation.

My dear Sir,

Your letter, which I received this afternoon, needs no apology.... Not to keep you in suspense, I will at once reply to your four questions as I may at the moment, intending to write again, if anything more satisfactory occurs to me, and requesting you very sincerely to write to me without scruple, as much and as often as it may seem good for your relief, on these serious and painful subjects. You may depend on my not betraying your confidence.

Now for your first point.... I have been used to think that, not the Church of England exclusively, but the Catholic Church throughout the world, had the *promises* of the Gospel confined to its pale, yet without prejudice to the notion that God's mercies might overflow, towards those especially, who, trying to do their best in their position, are kept from believing merely by invincible ignorance. And this I believe to be the doctrine of all parts of the Church, and of the Church of Rome quite as decidedly as of any other. Of course we are inadequate judges both of the degree in which people try to do their best, and of what is invincible ignorance ; and from the unhappy divisions of the Church, now

for many centuries, we are also but poor judges who
are, or are not, within her pale. My own impression
is, that the three great divisions of Rome, Greece, and
England are (at least I hope so) within the pale.
Others, holding the Creed but not having the fellow-
ship of the Apostles, would seem to be in schism.
Deniers of the Creed, in whole or in part, in heresy.
Socinianism seems a very aggravated form of this,
no more entitled to call itself Christian, than the
teaching of Mahomet, who owned one God, and our
Lord to be His prophet.

2. I trust there is no reasonable doubt that the
Bishops and Priests of either of the three great
sections of the Church which I have mentioned, have
Christ's commission conveyed to them by imposition
of hands, for the offering and consecration of the
Holy Communion, and are, therefore, successors of
the Apostles as Christian Priests.

3. As to books to be read, I am not very fond of
urging the study of Evidences as such. But I should
recommend to all who have leisure, and will take the
trouble of thinking, that they should read and consider Bishop Butler's "Analogy," which contains the
*principles* of all belief; our assent to the several doctrines of the Gospel being but the application of
those principles.

I should earnestly advise any person who wished
to be well grounded in the truth, instead of reading
controversial books (unless his duty as a clergyman

or the like compelled him) to go on taking for granted that the doctrine of the Church was true, *and acting upon it.* I believe this to be, I will not say the *best*, but the *only* way to come to a real grasp of holy truths. Mr. Newman's Sermons will, I think, be of as much use as any book I know, in sustaining persons in such a resolute faith as this, and in removing occasional misgivings. I should, of course, assume the devotional rather than critical study of Holy Scripture itself: the Gospels especially.

4. Generally speaking, I should greatly deprecate such argumentation as you enquire about. Rather I would advise a person to retire into himself, and meet profane sayings by inward devotion; of course taking proper opportunities of shewing that he feels that kind of pain, which will hinder a kind or even a well-bred person from holding such language before him.

Your letter does not hint at any possibility of your withdrawing out of the reach of such distressing and (perhaps) perilous discourse. I presume, therefore, that circumstances make it impossible.

Excuse this very hasty answer to such serious questions: and believe me, dear Sir, with very sincere prayer that you may be safely guided through your difficulties,

Yours very truly,

J. KEBLE.

## LETTER XL.

### To the Same.

MY DEAR ——,

I have been wishing to write to you ever since I received your letter, but there has been rather a press of parochial business. And now, I fear, I shall seem to answer you rather briefly and abruptly, but you must not think it arises from want of interest, or from any wish to have fewer or shorter letters from you (for, believe me, your letters are most refreshing to me), but your questions this time involve so much, that if I were to enter into them at any length, I should be trying more than I have time for. So I will just send you my first and general impressions, and bear the matters in mind, should anything occur hereafter.     •

I see nothing that you can do in the very distressing sort of trial which you mention, but to shew yourself unmoved by it, as far as you are yourself concerned, and distressed as far as God's honour is touched ; and if this be accompanied with command of temper, and with scrupulous and earnest endeavours to be useful and agreeable in all innocent ways, I cannot but hope that you will before long begin to find your reward in some way or other ; the whole matter being of course committed to God by secret and diligent prayer, and that prayer commended by persevering endeavours to be holy.

Those who, professing to take Scripture literally, argue from what was said to Adam that there was no future state for him and his posterity, might be asked why they cannot take the sayings of the New Testament (S. John v. 28, and others equivalent to it) *as* literally : they surely speak more unequivocally.

But, perhaps, what was meant was (what Bishop Warburton, among others, I believe held), that if our Lord had not redeemed man, he *would* have perished by annihilation. This, I think, we may let pass, as a subtlety which no way concerns us.

The Roman controversy is one to which I feel myself altogether inadequate, for want both of reading and other qualifications, but my impressions are,

1. That we are bound to continue thankfully in that Branch of the Church in which Providence has placed us : and that, with a view to our doing so, it is best to avoid reading works such as this of Bishop Baines (which I never saw) probably is, written purposely to unsettle those out of Communion with Rome : indeed, I would say, avoid controversial reading generally, and employ yourself rather with what is devotional and practical.

2. And on the other side, I never could have much sympathy with those who dwell eagerly on the supposed errors of that Church. I cannot see why, under common circumstances, we may not be at once faithful to our own Communion, and neutral towards Rome. It seems to me an extraordinary stretch of

private judgment, for a private Christian to condemn either; and although no course unhappily is without difficulties, yet I trust that it may be found a safe way at the last, to go on where Providence has set one, labouring and praying, not controversially but practically, for that holiness which alone can truly unite men, and which, if generally revived, would no doubt bring back with it, visible unity. With regard to those two little books of mine, I know they are very superficial, and lay down the law far too positively for a person of so little reading as myself. I do not, therefore, advise you to trust them any further than you find them borne out by real good authorities.

Law's "Serious Call" is most admirable, but one must not quite swear by him, as he had sometimes a most curiously one-sided way of looking at a matter: of which you will find an instance in his advising every person to sing aloud, in church and in his room, whether with or without voice and ear.

As to the last and most serious part of your letter, I will say at once, that I know of no insuperable difficulty to hinder a person in your line of life from changing it, at some time, for Holy Orders—I have known instances of it; nor do I see any reason, from what you tell me of your own case, why you should discard the thought to which you seem to have been in some sense providentially guided; only do not so dwell upon it, as to make the disappointment too

severe, should anything happen to hinder it altogether ; nor yet so as to make you less active and
conscientious in your present calling. In short, keep
it in mind as a thing possible, and as a thought which
should help you to be more and more circumspect
in all your efforts to please God, but still as a very
doubtful matter, and one in which you are rather
to wait for the leadings of Divine Providence, than
to form decided plans for yourself.

I hope it will not be long before you will find it
possible to speak on this matter to some one connected with yourself, and so having more right and
ability to judge than I have.

Believe me, dear ———,

With best wishes,

Yours affectionately,

J. KEBLE.

P.S. Thank you very much for remembering me,
as in the last sentence of your letter. I have much
need of all the good prayers that can be made
for me.

## LETTER XLI.

### To the Same : Hints on Self-guidance.

My dear ———,

It is so rare in our profession to find oneself treated
with real confidence, especially by young persons,

G

that when such a thing does happen, one feels quite
refreshed by it: for my sake, therefore, as well as
your own, let me beg of you to address me and tell
me things without scruple, as long as I can be of any
use to you, or to any one for whom you are in-
terested. I do not wonder at the feeling you express
to me of dread as to what may happen by and by,
when your situation is a more dangerous one, nor at
your almost seeming as if you were a hypocrite in
your correspondence with me. We are, almost all
of us, such double-minded persons, our best moments
so miserably unlike our worst, that it is but natural
we should sometimes feel so, and then our enemy
will endeavour to make us think it is all over with
us, at least for the present, and that we may just as
well be consistent, at least for a time, in pursuit of
present enjoyment; but let me beg of you not to
listen to him, but rather to the good angels who
would make you consistent the other way.

Perhaps, left as you are to yourself, it may help
you towards this happy result, if you keep, at least
for a time, some sort of register of your advances or
relapses in those matters on which your conscience
most troubles you: something very brief, only just
sufficient to help the memory, and if it were in short-
hand, or some kind of cypher, so that, even if mislaid,
it might betray nothing, this would lessen one objection to the practice.

You might try it, at least for a time, say a week
or a month, and see how it answers.

I am in good hope that when you go to reside in London, you will find more help than you now perhaps fancy. I may perhaps be able to help you with introductions, if you let me know when you are going. In the meantime be of good heart, and never permit your mind to indulge in any kind of despondency. Our Lord's rule, "Take no thought for the morrow," may well be applied to this matter, as well as to others merely temporal.

I do not wonder at what you say of poor Blanco White's book ; it is just what I should expect from all that I have heard of it, and remember of him. I understand that it strikes persons who knew him well, and who are otherwise best able to judge, as being simply infidel and unchristian.

Jones's is a very good little book. I suppose the reason of its not being reprinted may be, that of late that controversy has not been very rife, *as a controversy.* I do not know the Natural History of Religion.

I shall be glad if anything happens before long to bring us into personal acquaintance with each other, though I have an uncomfortable consciousness that you would find me very different from what your imagination tells you. Could not you give me a line beforehand whenever you go to ——, and go or come back our way. Do think of it, and

Believe me always

Your faithful and affectionate friend,

J. KEBLE.

## LETTER XLII.

To the Same, on Loneliness and lack of Sympathy.

You must not be too much cast down by the sort
of ill-feeling which you seem to perceive in those
around you, since you have tried to realise your convictions more thoroughly.  Provided we guard against
pride and rash judgment, I suppose such things may
even be thankfully accepted as an additional ground
for hoping that one is, so far, in the right.

Certainly it is a deep and real addition to your
trials that you have no one near to whom you can
at all speak freely on the matters nearest your heart.
But it must be borne, like bereavements of all kinds,
with patience, its contingent ill effects, such as you
describe, watched and prayed against, and I make
no question that in this way it will surely, and not
very slowly, be turned into a blessing.  One great
possible advantage of it I seem to discern, that it
even forces a serious person to have root in himself,
instead of leaving him in danger of relying too much
on the one, two, or three, whom he might feel that
he could trust.

It is a severe discipline, the loneliness in which you
are placed ; but if met manfully and in the fear of
God, I suppose it to be singularly calculated to es-
tablish a high and noble character, higher and nobler

than could be easily formed in more comfortable circumstances.

One thing occurs to me as a possible help in soothing and relieving your pent-up feelings, viz. that you should, if circumstances allow, get into a regular course of some kind of charitable visiting among poor and distressed people.

Music heard and practised, poetry read and written, drawing, scenery, gardening, and all kinds of out-of-door recreations, if not too exciting, may be made useful in this way, but the *specific* is works of charity and devotion.

I hope I shall soon hear from you again ; and again I beseech you, do not fear writing either too often or too long.

Believe me always

Affectionately yours,

J. KEBLE.

P.S. I quite enter into what you say of your first placing where you are, and should be sorry if the words of that Sermon were felt as blaming such arrangements indiscriminately. I suppose I meant them as cautionary. But I was, and am, quite unfit and unworthy to pass censure on any one.

## LETTER XLIII.

### TO A FRIEND UNDER DISAPPOINTMENT.

MY VERY DEAR ——,

Forgive my not writing sooner. It is not through forgetfulness, for, indeed, my thoughts are very much with you, and so it is with us all, whom you have trusted with what was in your heart. It is, indeed, a real calamity, a heavy burthen which you are called on to bear; but in it, as in all other ills, we are mercifully permitted and invited to "make a virtue of necessity." As one tells the poor people, most truly, that their involuntary fasts, patiently acquiesced in, will be accepted as voluntary sacrifices, so (and much more, in proportion to the completeness of the sacrifice, and the greatness of the pain) will it be in this case.

I wish some of us could have been with you in your journey home, which must have been, humanly speaking, so dreary: but as we know Who was with you, so I should not wonder if you had much comfort that we cannot know of. As I write, it strikes me that the prayer in Thomas à Kempis, bk. iii. c. 29*,

* "Blessed be Thy Name, O Lord, for ever ; for that it is Thy will that this temptation and tribulation should come upon me.

"I cannot escape it, but must needs flee unto Thee, that Thou mayest help me, and turn it to my good.

"Lord, I am now in affliction, and it is not well with me, but I am much troubled with the present suffering.

especially the application in it, of St. John xii. 27,
is particularly suited to this kind of trial.   May you
be helped, and I somehow feel sure that you will
be helped, to make much of it, and of such like
thoughts.

## LETTER XLIV.

### To One in Distress for past Sin, and on Remedies against Temptation.

My dear ——,

If you knew my real history, you would know
how little it would become such an one to turn

"And now, O beloved Father, what shall I say? I am in a strait;
save Thou me from this hour.

"Yet therefore came I unto this hour, that Thou mightest be glori-
fied, when I shall have been greatly humbled, and by Thee delivered.

"Let it please Thee, Lord, to deliver me; for, wretched that I
am, what can I do, and whither shall I go without Thee?

"Grant me patience, O Lord, even now in this my strait.  Help
me, my God, and then I will not fear, how grievously soever I be
afflicted.

"II. And now in these my troubles, what shall I say?

"Lord, Thy will be done!  I have well deserved to be afflicted and
grieved.

"Surely I ought to bear it; and O that I may bear it with patience,
until the tempest be overpast, and all be well again, or even better!

"But Thine omnipotent Hand is able to take even this temptation
from me, and to assuage the violence thereof, that I utterly sink not
under it; as oftentimes heretofore Thou hast done unto me, O my God,
my mercy!

"And the more difficult it is to me, so much the more easy to Thee
is this change of the right Hand of the Most High."—*Imitation*, bk. ii.
§ 29.—(Ed.)

away from a frail and erring brother; and were I,
indeed, such as you mistakenly imagine, it would
be the very joy of my heart to welcome and encourage the penitent.   I do not mean to make light
of the sad account you sent me : the fall, no doubt,
has been grievous, and you do well to judge and
condemn yourself for it, but do not for a moment
despond.   Set yourself to the work of penitence as
you would to the cure of any bodily illness : judge
and punish yourself secretly and soberly for the
fault, and watch with all your might against every
degree of relapse, especially guarding (as our Lord
Himself directed) the eyes.   I suppose no words can
express the importance of that one caution.

If evil thoughts occur in the night, rise and pray
on your knees for a few moments : say, e.g. the
51st Psalm.   Some *slight* bodily hardship is often
useful, I believe, at such times.   Be very careful
about your fasting, whether in the way of penitence
or precaution; it causes sometimes, especially when
persons are unused to it, a kind of reaction very
distressing.   If you have reason to fear that, you
had better use hard and unpleasant diet, instead
of actually going without.

If you find that your mind is still oppressed, and
especially if your enemy still haunts you, make use
of the Church's motherly direction about confession.
You will find directions for it, and for the conduct of your repentance altogether, in a little book

lately republished, Kettlewell's "Companion for the Penitent."

Pray do not give up your intention of coming to see us; there is one person in the house, at any rate, who ought to be very thankful to be allowed to kneel down and ask pardon with you ; one who has need of all the help he can find for himself, and to whom, therefore, it is the greatest charity to shew him how he may be of some little help to others. I quite depend upon making your acquaintance some day. God grant we may meet in peace ; and we shall do so, if we meet as true penitents.

Ever yours affec<sup>ly</sup>,

J. KEBLE.

## LETTER XLV.

### REMEDIES AND HELPS UNDER TEMPTATION.

MY DEAR ——,

It was a great relief to hear from you again, sad as your report is in some respects : for I had begun to fear that I had lost you quite : I mean, that I was to give up the hope which I had entertained, and in which I found a peculiar sort of comfort, that I, unworthy as I know myself to be, might be permitted to do you good. Your writing again is a merciful token, that both you and I may have hope for ourselves and for one another ; I trust I am not wrong in saying this with entire confidence.

If the Great Judge had already sentenced you, He would not put it into your mind to have such misgivings, and to write so of yourself to one, to whom you are drawn no otherwise than as to His (supposed) instrument for your good. No, my dear young friend, be sure you are very very dear to Him. He is but waiting to see you stand manfully in His strength (which you will have if you pray for it) against the next assault of your enemy: you know you *can* do it, if you will — you have that power, for how would it be if some one were by who stood in some very dear and sacred relation to you, a parent for example, or a sister? Should you not of course keep *then* from outward excess at least, such as they could take notice of? Only in this case you must not wait for outward excess: the time to think of God's eye being upon you is when your own eyes are tempted to look the wrong way, or your ears to listen to what you know will prove near occasions of sin ; it is there, where the battle of purity must be fought, and where the purity of Repentance must begin to be recovered, even if that of innocency is lost.

In other words, the only safety in temptations, properly called carnal, is in *flight ;* when that can be had, it is vain trusting to resistance. This you will find strongly put in a little book called the "Spiritual Combat," which has been translated, and edited by Dr. Pusey ; there are many things in it which I think may be useful to you.

I cannot but hope something from your being called home just now; family anxiety (for I will hope it may not amount to affliction) and absence for a while from the scene of your usual temptations, seem providential calls, of which a good use may be made. I would beg of you to watch every thing of that sort, every thing that tends to recall you to your better self, however trifling or merely accidental it may seem.

You are, if I do not guess wrongly, sensitive and quick in your imaginations, and able, therefore, to catch up and to interpret every hint of that kind which your ever-present Friend may vouchsafe you. The mere exercise of watching for such hints will do you good, by God's blessing, in many ways.

Do you know La Motte Fouqué's "Sintram and his Companions?" if you do not, I would beg you to get it and read it; it will explain what I mean in· these last sentences, which perhaps may be rather obscure.

I should repeat to you now, more earnestly than ever, the advice I gave, about avoiding disputes and mere conversations on sacred subjects. You seem yourself quite aware of the danger, and perhaps it behoves you more than ever to think of others, who might be injured by one's conversing on such subjects, without earnest preparation of the heart and conduct.

In the mean time, be of good courage, I beseech you, in this respect also; make it specially matter of your prayers, and assure yourself that here, as in the other equally painful subject, it is not having a bad thought suggested to you, but consenting to it, which makes guilt before God.

If the worst comes to the worst, and you find yourself so tempted in your present situation that you cannot *fight*, you have still the chance of *flying*, that is, of sacrificing your present prospects; if you could so do it as to punish yourself only, it might be an acceptable offering, and obtain a great blessing.  But I say this, of course, in great ignorance, and in much doubt whether I ought to say it at all; only that this, or indeed anything would be better than going on in a bad way, in a kind of reckless despondency.

If anything more occurs to me, I will write to you again, for, indeed, I think of you daily : but I deeply wish you had some one at hand whom you might trust in these matters.  Yet, again, you have such an One at hand ; only fear not to trust Him.  And never, never give way to despair.  Think of the good Angels and Saints praying for you, and of your friends who are gone ; and think of one most unworthy, who depends partly on you, to "cover the" sad "multitude of his sins."

Ever anxiously and affectionately yours,

J. KEBLE.

## LETTER XLVI.

To the Same: Practical Hints and Suggestions as
to Behaviour towards a Sceptical Friend.

My dear young Friend,

I must thank you over and over for the joy and
comfort which your letter has given me, for, indeed,
I was afraid that I might not hear from you again,
and did not know where you might have wandered:
but I have never, I believe, gone for a day without thinking of you, and that I now receive such
a letter from you, I cannot but be very thankful.
To be sure it does not look much like thankfulness
to have gone on for near three weeks without re-
plying. But in good truth we have been very busy
here. . . . There has also been an unusual number of
deaths in the village: and I have gone on hoping
that I might write more satisfactorily. But it will
not do to wait any longer, and I must answer your
very interesting applications as I can.

My answer, I think, will come to this; that if
I could make your personal acquaintance, I should
be much better able to give you an opinion, both
as to your London life, and as to the course to be
pursued with your young friends about whom you
consult me.

With regard to the first, the notions which I have
are so very vague and general, that I really do not

know how to give advice.   But if we could converse
a little, face to face, something definite and useful
might possibly turn up.   You know, of course, that
young men have now opportunities, more than they
had, of attending the Services of the Church, and, as
I trust, more sympathy among one another, in their
endeavours to be good or penitent.   Indeed, I suppose that you would be able to secure thorough
spiritual guidance of a truly Catholic sort in London,
if you could make up your mind to apply for, and
act upon it.   In the mean time, I hope that you will,
without scruple, make any use that you can of me,
only bearing with my tardy and scanty replies, and
believing, as the truth is, that it is, in one sense,
a great comfort, and in another a very useful lesson
to me, to receive such applications.

I wish I could see my way more clearly in advising
you with regard to that other most sacred matter.
The principles, I suppose, of all such enquiries are
to be found in Bishop Butler's " Analogy ;" but to
apply them to this, or any other special point of
Theology, may require deeper thought than you can
expect, in such a young person as you mention.

Yet if a man can bring himself to study the Bible
reverentially, I confess it does appear to me, that the
Unity of the Godhead on the one hand, and on the
other, the claim of our Lord to be loved and trusted
in *as God*, are both so expressly set forth, as to make
the Arian hypothesis *prima facie* untenable.   And

so I expect it will be found again, as it always seems to have been found after no long time, though it may revive more or less among the confusions of this generation, of which I think I see symptoms, besides what you report.

Of course one must suppose the happiest way would be, if such an one as your friend could submit himself unreservedly to the Church's teaching in the Creeds, making experiment of it by a holy life. But if he cannot bring himself to that, I know nothing in the way of argumentative reading that I can recommend better than Bishop Pearson, especially on the second Article. (I suppose he is a scholar.) If he is a metaphysician, I could almost think that part of S. Augustine on the Trinity might prove interesting, and help to satisfy him. But I really wish you could come here, if it were but for a day ... and we could talk over these things at our leisure.

Ever believe me,<br>
Yours affectionately,<br>
J. KEBLE.

## LETTER XLVII.

### To the Same.

My dear ——,

We hope to be at home again the end of next week, and shall be very happy to see you at any

time afterwards that may be convenient to you. . . .
It will be a real pleasure to make your personal
acquaintance, and to be permitted to hope that I
may be of use to you; but do not wait for that or
anything else in making good rules and trying to
keep them. I fear you will find things at Hursley
very different from what you probably in your kindness expect; but the good rules I speak of are the
same everywhere, and within your reach always.

I should recommend you, if you can, to make yourself contented with your Parish Church, disregarding
what you perceive to be contrary to the Prayer-book,
and taking whatever is doubtful in the best sense.

Those who know better than I do seem to think
this the right course in such cases, now, alas! too
common.

Believe me,
Yours always very truly,
J. KEBLE.

## LETTER XLVIII.

### To the Same, on Confession.

My dear young Friend,

Indeed I am very sorry for you, but I must not
lose a moment in beseeching you not to despair, but
to go on courageously in the way of penitence, on
which, by God's grace, you have entered. I feel sure

that as the evil spirit must have rejoiced in your fall (no doubt he was especially busy with you, those who are making any kind of effort in the way of goodness must always expect to find him so), so the good Angels rejoiced, and I trust are still rejoicing, at your having the heart to confess. May He, who put that good mind into you, strengthen you more and more by His grace, that you may feel more and more the shame and horror of so dealing with the members of Christ, and resolve more and more earnestly, to avoid not only the sin, but all temptations and near occasions of it, however dull and wearisome the time may seem to pass to you. The dulness and weariness, as far as they go, will be useful in the way of penance.

I forget whether I mentioned to you, in talking of this kind of subject, that some people had found it useful to associate the idea of dirt, of bodily foulness and loathsomeness, with temptations of that sort. But I am persuaded that in most cases (and yours seems no exception) *regular* confession, and not ocsional only, will be found the best help, by way both of precaution and remedy. It was partly with this view that I mentioned to you Mr. ——, whom I suppose to be a most discreet and charitable director. But I hope you will understand that I am quite at your service, should you prefer "opening your grief" to me, Providence having somehow brought us together.

H

I think you had better begin immediately to prepare for what is called General Confession, by reviewing your whole history, and setting down your sins as well as you can ; any book of preparation for the Holy Communion will help you to do so. And, having this paper by you, you may add to it from time to time, as new faults occur, or old ones are remembered ; and then when a good opportunity comes, you may pour it all out into your loving Lord's ear, through some one of His unworthy Priests, and be by Him, through the Priest's mouth, so fully absolved, that the sins, if not returned to, shall be no more mentioned unto you, and you may with humble confidence communicate as often as ever you can reverently draw near. In the meantime, I should rather recommend your abstaining from Holy Communion, unless the time, from circumstances, were too long, in which case you should make your earnest purpose of special confession, when it may be had, part of your preparation for the Sacrament.

Pray consider this, and with earnest prayer. I cannot but hope that courage will be given you to try this remedy, bitter as it must be, and to persevere in it. You need not have to wait long, as, if you prefer Mr. —— (which, on many accounts, I should be glad of), you might go to him at any time. The practice once begun, I trust in His great goodness would go on, and do you great good. The general

confession need not be repeated, though you changed
your director, unless you wished it.

May He, who can, forgive and bless you,

And believe me always,

Your affectionate Friend,

J. KEBLE.

## LETTER XLIX.

### THE SAME SUBJECT CONTINUED.

YOUR letter was a great comfort to me, and I
earnestly hope and pray that you may not suffer
anything to move you from the course which you
have marked out for yourself. I am so sure it is the
right one. If I had plenty of time, I might, perhaps,
have much more to say on the best way of dis-
charging the duty you have now undertaken of
special confession. At present I will only just say,
be not too scrupulous in setting down things, nor yet
too general, but take some one or more as specimens
in any kind which may have become habitual, and
describe the frequency of the habit, if you can, by
the number of sins in a given time, and the degree,
by some aggravating circumstances, such as your
conscience most reproaches you for, and He who is
merciful will accept it, if fairly so intended, for a full
confession. What you write is best written in some
kind of cypher or abbreviation, lest it be lost, and do

harm.   Do it all as a religious exercise, as in God's presence, and a good deal on your knees.   Being thus set down as you may remember it, it will save you the trouble of recollection when you come to confess, and you will be more at leisure for pure contrition.

On the whole matter you will find good directions in Bishop Taylor's " Holy Dying," and " Golden Grove ;" and also in Kettlewell's " Companion to the Penitent."

May God and all good angels be with you in the good work.

## LETTER L.

My dear Miss ——,

How little do you know what sort of a person you are consulting, on so very sacred a matter ! but let that pass ; worthy or unworthy, my office binds me to do my best for a Christian person who thinks I can help him ; and it will be indeed a comfort, of which I am quite unworthy, if I am enabled to be of any use or consolation to you.   I cannot but be very thankful that the wish you mention should have been put into your Heart, and again, that you should have submitted it, in the manner you have done, to your parents ; this latter seems to me, if I may say so without presumption, one of the most comfortable tokens that the former was from God; and if so, it cannot of course be meant that it should pass away from your mind or memory; it must, as you instinctively feel, give a tone and colour to all your future life. Only there are two things to be guarded against; one, that so long as your parents are known to disapprove, it should not ripen into a positive purpose, or anything amounting to a vow; the other, that in shaping your course of life by it, there should be as little as possible for them to take notice of, in such a way as might pain them. But to you I need scarcely mention this. Indeed, whilst I write it occurs to me, that your having mentioned this subject to them may very much lessen the difficulty of your keeping any rules which you may find profitable for you. They can better enter into your feelings, and good may be done in many ways. I have only to add, that whatever other deficiencies you find in me (as indeed, among other things, I have scarcely any experience as a trusted adviser), at least I shall attend with deep interest to anything you may wish to say or write to me; and may God grant that I may be able to be of service to you, and not prove utterly unsuited to the aweful name of Spiritual Father.

May God bless you, for surely you are His dear child, and believe me,

(Always asking your prayers,)

Sincerely and affectionately yours,

J. KEBLE.

# LETTER LI.

## To the Same, on Management of Time, on Dress, Silence, &c.

My dear Miss ——,

.... I quite approve of your plan for making the most of your days and hours, with the understanding always that you do not bind yourself to it, so as to make it an entanglement, and that the part which relates to fasts and vigils be always modified as health shall seem to recommend. Concerning silence, dress, and ornaments, I can only think of one general caution, in addition to what you mention ; viz. to watch well one's likings and dislikes, whether they tend towards silence and plainness, or the contrary, and, in a gentle, unobtrusive kind of way, rather to contradict them than not ; I do not mean violently, for that would be unnatural and unreal, but just a little, and of course only in cases where obedience and other duties leave a choice.   I do not know that I have any more to say on your plan, except wishing it a most hearty God speed, and telling you what a comfort it is to me, as I go about the parish seeming to do no good, to think of you and other kind friends at a distance remembering one.

# LETTER LII.

## To a Person under Special Temptation.

I THINK it probable that some of your worst falls arise in some measure from your getting into an excited and irregular state of body and mind by sitting up late, whether for study or amusement, and that if you could set yourself a moderately strict rule in that matter, and keep to it, besides the little self-denial, it would be a help to you, in more ways than one. At the same time you know very well that there is one who will make it his particular business to put this sort of temptation in your way. . . . Therefore you must not be too much cast down, nor think all is going wrong, should you find yourself for a long time haunted in the way I mean: only do not lend yourself to it in the least degree, do not wait to fight, but fly; and perhaps it may help if you use yourself to consider it as specially a work of the devil, which no doubt it often is. If you can get your hours of sleeping and waking properly arranged, might you not, do you think, find time to say the fifty-first Psalm *before* your other prayers, the first thing on waking in the morning: and then if you *should* happen to wake in the night, it would suggest itself. Especially when the enemy seems near, it would be almost sure help, if you got up and prayed.

As to the bitter and scornful words, might it not be a good help against them to make a rule of trying to remember at such times something that you are most ashamed of. The very effort would do much good, though the thought were ever so rapid and superficial, and might scarce seem to amount to contrition.

I shall, I hope, pray for you, that your earnest wish for a like-minded companion may be granted, and that it may prove an effectual help in the way you wish. I think you should be aware that some of your trials are of that subtle nature that no society, nor state of life, nor anything else but the grace of God blessing one's sincere endeavours, can overcome them. So that, even if you had such a friend, some of the gravest of your trials might still continue : and by His gracious help you may be completely delivered without such an outward advantage. Only be resolute in guarding your thoughts and senses, and cleanness of heart will, by God's blessing, return ; and if I am not mistaken, this will help more than you might think in checking the bitter and angry thoughts and words which you complain of. For few things, I suppose, put a person more out of tune, than the feeling of continually yielding to what he is ashamed of, and what, in his better mind, he detests.

Ever yours very affectionately,

J. KEBLE.

# LETTER LIII.

## TO THE SAME.

I WILL mention two things which may help you.

1. Some penitents have found help in using themselves when they wake in the night to rise and say the fifty-first Psalm, with the latter part of the Commination Office.

2. All, penitents or not, may find help in fixing on one petition of the Lord's Prayer to be thought on specially each day in the week.

# LETTER LIV.

## TO A RELAPSED PENITENT.

FILI IN CHRISTO CARISSIME,

You may judge what a grief and disappointment to me was your report of yourself, though I was so far prepared for it as to have great misgivings in consequence of not hearing from you : still I own it is more distressing than I had hoped, and I am not sure, that, had I been at hand, I should have recommended so early an approach to the most holy things : perhaps I might, but it would have depended on tokens of which it is impossible to judge at a distance. But do not understand me as blaming you in the least, my dear young friend. I dare say

you did it for the best, and I trust that He has
blessed and will continue to bless it.  I think you
will do well to set yourself this rule, should you fall
in the same way again, at once to confess, and sus-
pend yourself from Communion, until you have my
answer ; not giving way to false shame, nor running
the chance of further relapses.  And in any case
might it not be well to send me a report of yourself
weekly ; though ever so summary, it might be better
than nothing.  Also, if I had seen you, I should
have asked you a little about the " near occasions "
(as they are called) of your relapses,—in the way
of place, company, books, enticing objects, whether
in the street or at home, and the best ways of
avoiding them.

We are sad children, and must deal cunningly
with ourselves ; and sometimes a very simple precaution, undertaken and kept in the fear of God,
and prayer, and as in the Presence of Christ, will
baffle a very deep and dangerous snare of the enemy.

As you are often hindered from the Church
prayers, it seems the more needful for you to practise repeating Psalms and saying short prayers to
yourself.  Sisters of Mercy do so in the streets, and
why should not Brothers of Penitence ?

Also, would it not be well to have something to
amuse your mind in walks and vacant hours, and
keep it out of mischief.  Especially let me beg of
you to be punctual in your self-examination, and if

you could meditate every morning for a short time on Eternity and something connected with it, on the Divine Presence, or on 1 Cor. vi. 19, and other such texts, until you found yourself in a way to offer earnestly such a resolution as I will enclose herewith, I trust you would find yourself gradually released from the sad chain which has wound itself round you. This is all that occurs to me at present. Let me hear very soon ; and believe me,

Now as ever,

Your very affec<sup>te</sup> and anxious,

J. K.

# LETTER LV.

## To the Same, on Confession and Communion.

I HAVE a mingled feeling from your last note ; great pain at what it tells of one thing, yet thankfulness to hear of so much (surely we may humbly say so) general improvement. With regard to Holy Communion, I believe, according to the exact rules of the Churches that require auricular confession, you ought not to participate again before absolution. But I consider that English Priests are not only permitted, but commanded, to leave to their penitents a certain discretion with regard to those rules. You must use the best of your judgment, with prayer, and strict watchfulness during the remainder of this

week, and if you then heartily in conscience think
it best to communicate on Sunday, I trust that by
His grace you will be right. To be quite exact,
I suppose you would have to confess to ——, or
some other Clergyman, orally, all serious falls that
you could remember since you were absolved, and
seek fresh absolution and direction. But I repeat
that according to English rules, as I understand
them, this may be dispensed with. Only be very
very careful that your being spared this humiliation
prove not a fresh occasion of falling.


# LETTER LVI.

## To the Same.

YOUR letter is most welcome, and a great comfort
to me in two ways especially.

1. How thankful we ought to be to Almighty
God for preserving you in your main trial, and for
enabling you on the whole (I trust we may say) to
win some ground.

2. I am glad to know what you now tell me of
your circumstances, how that your remaining in your
present line of life is in some sort a continued act
of self-denial. Trying as it must be, it is so far
satisfactory, as it is a penance enjoined on you by
God Himself, and if so taken and acknowledged,
I doubt not that by His blessing it will help in the

work of penance, and tend towards making repentance complete and effectual. Will you think of it so in your devotions, and ask for that particular blessing on your day's work? So undertaken, it will surely prosper in that whereunto He sends it; and in His good time, if He sees it best, He may call you to His more immediate service.

I hardly know what to recommend you for Holy Week, pressed as you are with business; but perhaps Isaac Williams's book with that title may be as good a help to meditation as any you can find. Do not read on too glibly, but pause on it when any affecting thought occurs, so as to make it meditation in earnest. And if you can keep the hours of prayer with any good little book (e. g. Christie's "Day Hours,") it may be of good use.

And now may God bless you with all the blessings of this good time, and grant you entire victory over His and your enemies. In Him I hope to be,

Yours always affectionately,<br>J. KEBLE.

## LETTER LVII.

### To the Same: Rules for Self-government.

My dear ——,

I must write one line, if it be only to say, never scruple about writing to me under the notion of my

being busy. I scarce know what could be of more
consequence to me than helping such work as I trust
you are now thoroughly engaged in, be it only by
affording you a means of relieving your mind. It
seems to me that the sort of frequent report you have
sent me of late may be of great use to you, and
I would say by no means discontinue it. (I destroy
your little papers, when I have read and considered
them.) By the blessing of Him to whom this season
belongs, I trust you have been making real use of
it. This last report comforts me again. Only be
in one sense more on your guard when the instinctive restraint of the penitential time is over. Be
sure there will be a re-action, if not averted by special grace, for which I hope you will pray.

The watching of your temper will be a hard fight,
but not a hard plan of operations. Do you think
you could get into a way of calling up a contrite
thought of whatever you are most ashamed of when
anything affronts you? If you could subdue pride
and anger by contrition for evil desire, this would
be killing two or three birds with one stone. The
doubting thoughts probably come from the quarter
you suggest. They cannot be much of your own
since they take such opposite directions. Would
it not be best to try and put them down as you
would any other bad thoughts? I was foolish about
Isaac Williams's book; I meant that on the Passion,
and forgot there were two.

With my most sincere Easter benediction, such as it is, believe me, dear son in Christ,

Y<sup>r</sup> ever affec<sup>te</sup>,

J. K.

## LETTER LVIII.

### To the Same, on the same Subject.

My dear ——,

I have just been reading over your last note, and will now say what occurs to me about the society of your old friends as constituting a near occasion of sin. May you not adopt a middle course between entire separation and going along with them in ill. By all means keep your good resolutions of keeping from the *place*, whatever it be, which you have found so dangerous, and be not afraid or ashamed to let your friends know, that, for reasons which seem to you good, you have made such a rule; keep steadily but good humouredly to it, and let them have their laugh at you if they will; and be also on the watch for occasions to oblige them innocently, and give up your own wishes to them in other little indifferent things. I shall be much surprised if the coldness you speak of do not soon pass away. If not, bear it quietly as a little penance, and be sure that you can do nothing really more unkind to them, as well as to yourself, than by swerving from your good rules in compliment to them.

Another point in your last note appears to me

very much to be thought of, where you say, you seemed to yourself to be "acting under some powerful agency," &c. Surely this feeling is providential, to warn you who it is that assails you so restlessly. Depend upon it, that being cannot bear to see your earnest beginnings of penitence, and it is not without him that such backslidings take place, and the next thing that he tries is to get people to give up in despair; but do not you let him, even for a quarter of an hour, get such dominion over you. Say a short prayer; use the sign of the crqss; exorcise him in the Saving Name, or in that into which you were baptized, and fear not but he will retire discomfited, and after a time you will not have help only, but peace. Only do not depend on that peace, but fear and suspect yourself, and pray very often against that special danger.

The moroseness of temper which you sometimes complain of, may in part be due to the same cause, and may be profitably met in the same way. Whatever you do, never doubt that He is always most willing to receive you on true repentance, and that the first trouble in that way is always the least. I mean that all delay only makes the pain greater.

If by such rules and thoughts as these you still find yourself unable to keep your ground steadily, it may be worth considering whether you would do well to open your mind to Mr. ——, or some other Priest on the spot, going to him immediately, as the

"Spiritual Combat" advises, after every serious transgression, to confess and be directed with regard to Holy Communion. The general confession made to me need not in that case be repeated, any more than might be necessary to give him a proper notion of the case; but every deadly sin since the last confession, should, as nearly as may be, be specified.

Believe me always,

Your affectionate Fatherly Friend,

J. KEBLE.

## LETTER LIX.

### To the Same : Rules of Penitence and Self-Protection.

My dear ——,

I was longing to hear from you, and am very glad you have written : though of course it is a deep grief that you can make no better a report. Indeed and indeed, my dear son in our Lord (as you encourage me to call you), your case is a very anxious one ; the frequent relapses seem to indicate, that the view taken of it at first was hardly so serious as it should have been. Do you not yourself think, that you ought now for penance to impose upon yourself a pretty long abstinence from Holy Communion, in short not to venture there again until you are regularly absolved ? and I suppose it would

I

be wrong to absolve without proof of penitence by
long abstinence from open and deliberate sin of that
kind.   And do not think that this is beyond your
power : you *know* that you can, if you will earnestly
try, as in God's Presence, and with prayer to Him,
you *can* resist and overcome temptations : you *can*
look another way : you *can* stay in doors after night,
when no business calls you out : you *can* hold your
tongue from accosting those whom you ought not :
you *can*, being awake at night, rise and kneel on
the floor and say a prayer, instead of permitting
yourself to be carried away by waking dreams of sin.
However, I am not now writing an answer to your
letter.   I have not time just now, but I was anxious
to say a word or two now at your return to ——.
It seems somewhat providential that you should
change your abode there just now, and as the old
abode led into mischief, so let us hope, that, by the
blessing of God, you may turn over a new leaf in
the new one.   By no means renew the intimacy
which you speak of, under any specious fancy which
may suggest itself to your mind of doing good to
the other party.   *Flight* is the approved remedy in
such cases.   Keep your distance and pray for her
and for yourself.   And whatever you do, do not go
boasting of your sin, nor be ashamed to be and to
seem (so far as you must seem anything) penitent.
Use the solitude which you dread as a penance, and
get some professional friend to set you a task of

professional reading, which, if you are indolently inclined, may in some sort answer the same purpose. And try and remember what sort of observances, quasi-penitences, and other precautions, seemed to do you most good in times past, when your repentance seemed most real, and go back to them now; the very recurrence, besides its other uses, will help to make you contrite. Perhaps you will kindly tell me what has seemed to answer best with you in this way, and I will endeavour to think if anything more can be done. As to the two violent remedies you speak of, I fear that neither of them would be an effectual remedy, except the heart could be changed. Do not dream of such things, but employ yourself; pray regularly, *keep early hours* (I suspect this is of great consequence), and meet each temptation as it occurs valiantly, using yourself to consider that your Enemy is present in person, if you could see him, and that your Lord is yet more present. Among writers, it strikes me that Bishop Taylor will help as much as any : but never forget that in this war flying is better soldiership than fighting. Do what good you can : the prayers of those whom you *help*, and of those whom you *forgive*, will be a great thing for you. I hope I shall soon write again : meantime accept my blessing such as it is.

Ever your anxious and loving,

J. K.

# LETTER LX.

## To an Unbaptized Lady desirous of Baptism, but whose Parents were opposed to it.

My dear Madam,

Indeed your letter required no apology. Even if it were not the duty of us all to do what we can to shew the way to a fellow-traveller, I. can truly say that it has filled me with interest, as it must any one who has not the heart of a stone. I only wish that I was more certain of being able to give you the best advice, but He to Whom and through Whom you (I am sure) pray continually, will I trust help me.

You have described your case so fully and clearly that one feels greatly helped in forming an opinion, and I will tell you at once the conclusion to which I have come: premising that not being myself a Father, and feeling that it would be a great confirmation or correction of my own view to have an independent opinion from one who is so, and having, by God's goodness, a clerical friend close at hand, of whom I will only say, that if you knew him you would, I think, have gone to him in preference to all others, I took the great liberty of laying your case before him, of course confidentially (I hope I was not wrong in this; he has a large family of sons and daughters, some of them grown up), and

I this morning received his opinion quite in unison with my own.

We think, 1. that you cannot go on as you are; God's providence clearly calls upon you to make your profession. 2. It can only be that profession to which in your mind and conscience you adhere, and towards which it appears that He has been silently and graciously leading you. Any other would be untrue in itself, and the appearance of any other would be a kind of scandal in various ways. This consideration seems to us to make one of your alternatives impossible, viz. the receiving Dissenters' Baptism under protest. I do not say that such baptism might not be valid; there is no need, I think, to discuss that question, because, how valid soever, you will, I think, perceive on reconsideration, that there would be a sort of painful unreality in it which would hardly bear reflection afterwards. It would be voluntary schismatical baptism, which would require to be healed, as it were, by confirmation, and in order to be healed, must be repented of and confessed as a fault. Nor can I think that it would really satisfy your father. Such as you describe him, he would be particularly alive to the unreality of it, and if it were sanctioned by one of us, it might prove a fresh ground of offence.

3. On the other hand, it seems very undesirable to go elsewhere and take such a serious step unknown to your parents, or only apprising them of

it afterwards. It has an air of undutifulness, mistrust, and concealment, which ought by all means
to be avoided if possible.

It remains 4. as the most advisable course, that
you should take some good opportunity and method
of opening your mind to your parents, directly or
through another, in speech or in writing, as you
may be led to think best.

You might say to them quite firmly, but with all
meekness and dutifulness, that you have gradually,
and as you believe providentially, been brought
into this mind, adding such details as may seem
to you fit and discreet; that your mind is (please
God) made up; you cannot be happy unbaptized,
and you feel that it would be a false and profane
thing for you to be baptized into any communion
saving that of the Church of England. If your
father receives this as you apprehend, it seems to
us that you would best do your duty both to him
and to your Heavenly Father, by giving him to
understand that you will be content to wait awhile,
and not press for immediate baptism, in hope that
he may reconsider his objections.

This would be but fair to him, even if he were
less likely to be keen and somewhat stern in his
opposition: considering how suddenly the thing will
come upon him, and from what point of view he
must unavoidably see it at first.

Well, this will probably cause a delay for an indefinite time in your obtaining your heart's desire; but you must not be broken-hearted, nor too anxious. You may comfort yourself with recollecting for how long a time, for months and years not unseldom, the baptism of many has been providentially deferred, on whom, nevertheless, God's blessing evidently rested. According to ancient discipline, you yourself might have been submitted to long probation, as a catechumen, most likely from now until Easter at least; and if it seemed hard, you would have quieted yourself with the thought that it was God's discipline, God's doing, and to be sure He would not permit you to be a loser by quietly submitting to it. Quiet yourself, my dear young lady, now with the like thought, and spend the weeks or months of delay, in earnest preparation for the unspeakable gift. If they should be years, they will be nothing as compared with its greatness.

After a time—who knows—you may even gain your father, or at least gain his not uncheerful permission, when he saw you thus walking before God and him in faith and humbleness. Should it be otherwise, He whom you wish to serve will answer your prayers, and shew you when, and how, to come to His Baptism.

Should it be His will to call you suddenly out of this world, so suddenly that even at the last moment you could not be baptized — your being taken away in the midst of such a course, with full desire and prayer for baptism, the Church and the Saints of God have always held that in such case He accepts the will for the deed.

Of course I do not mean that if, after a fair allowance of time, you see no chance of obtaining your parents' leave, you ought not (under further advice and with much prayer) to act for yourself, being of the age you are, and in the mind in which you would then be known to be.

My dear young friend, my heart aches for you, and I cannot say what comfort it will be, if, as I am in good hope, you shall be enabled to tell me one day, that the course which my friend and myself have thus ventured to recommend, has been blessed by your peacefully attaining what your soul longs for. But whether we hear of it in this world or no, if it be the course of faith and patience, its blessing will come only the more surely for being delayed.

One word more. It is probable that in your circumstances one great part of your trial will be to hear things, which with all your heart you love and reverence, evil-spoken of: and you will be tempted may be, at times, to speak and think the worst of Dissenters, as such, and of their ways. Force yourself, I beseech you, rather to keep silence, unless there be some grave duty in speaking; and to be glad, really glad, when you can speak and think well of them. Carry this rule out—you will want all helps to steady you in the Holy Church, troubled as it is with so many sad divisions; and this rule of "not rejoicing in iniquity, but rejoicing in the truth," i.e. in others' truth and goodness, will go a great way, please God, in keeping you right, imperfect as you will find many things.

Commending you to the Good Shepherd, I remain, in Him,

Y' faithful servant,

J. KEBLE.

## LETTER LXI.

To a Lady, on being informed of the Death of her Sister, the Widow of a Personal Friend of his own.

Dear Miss ——,

Your letter just received is, indeed, a trouble and a surprise to me; yet when I think again, why should we be troubled or surprised that He who is Love, and giveth Love, should not suffer those whom He had made happy together, and who, we trust (humanly speaking), were in His sight lovely in their lives, to be long divided in their deaths?

The shortness of the notice in itself would be indeed startling—but what a notice is widowhood itself! and it is a deep comfort to think of a sister, and of such a friend as —— being with her at the time.

The thoughts and sayings of dear N. concerning

those out of sight were always such as to make one almost involuntarily picture to oneself what meetings there must be in Paradise; and now (D.V.) it is with him no more an imagination, but a blessed reality. God grant us all to be ready when our time, which is near, shall come.

Accept my sincere thanks for remembering me at such a time, and believe me,

Dear Miss ——,

Your obliged and affectionate servant,

J. KEBLE.

# LETTER LXII.

### To a Young Lady, on Distractions, &c.

MY DEAR CHILD, (for so your letter even forces me to call you,)

. . . . I should like you to look at a little book which you may perhaps have, "Aids to a Holy Life," by a Mr. Bund. . . . Your failure of recollection in church is no new nor rare thing. In some respects it may be perhaps mended by mechanical helps— something equivalent to a Rosary as a kind of *memoria technica.* And you will remember Bp. Taylor's advice, to gather up as it were all the meaning of the lost prayer into a hearty Amen at the end of it. Remember this too, (which is in all the books, and I have no doubt it is quite true), that the hearty desire to be contrite is accepted as contrition, the hearty desire to believe as Faith, &c. In case anything should happen to hinder my coming, . . . . I will now give you just this one direction. Some time when you can best do it, before your next Holy Communion, say the Lord's Prayer, the Collect "Almighty God unto whom all hearts be open," and then, on your knees, tell our Lord (who of course is always with us,) what you have told me in this letter, with anything else which you would wish to tell, and earnestly beseech Him to bless this Communion to you, in the particular way which you feel the want of,—steady methodical efforts after self-knowledge and devotion. This may be inserted in your usual nightly confession, or may be tried at any other time, as you may find convenient.

God bless you, my dear Child.

Your affec<sup>te</sup> old friend,

J. K.

## LETTER LXIII.

### To a Lady, on Punishment of Sin, Free-Will, and other Religious Difficulties.

THE subject on which you have written to me, is indeed a very aweful and mysterious one ; and when followed up by an enquiring mind may easily bring with itself misgivings and perplexities, nay, perhaps it must do so, for is it not a part of the unanswer-

able question, How should there be any evil at all
in God's world? But taken simply as it stands in
Scripture, and as it is received by simple unrefining
persons, especially when they are called on themselves to endure God's chastening, it seems to approve itself to our natural and Christian instincts,
to be indeed part of the faith which we profess when
we call God our Father. "For what son is he whom
a father chasteneth not?" and is not chastening
punishment? When a mother puts her child to pain
for some fault which she wishes to correct, we call
it properly punishment, though it proceeds entirely
from love. But parental love is but the shadow of
Divine. Therefore I suppose that the sentiment one
hears so often from the sick poor, " I trust and pray
to have my punishment in this world, and not in
the next," is founded on truth and piety. Nor do
I see how it at all interferes with the only All-suffi-
cient Virtue of the Cross. These sufferings are, in
one way, the Father's mode of applying the Cross
to us, as His Sacraments are in another way.

I hope that in the passage to which you allude,
which I suppose to be in page 62, you will find
nothing inconsistent with this.

You seem to think that the fulness of our Lord's
Atonement excludes all notion of temporal punishment to be laid on those for whom it is made,
but you do not allege words or facts of Scripture,
only it seems to you to follow from the doctrine that

"the punishment demanded by God's justice for the sins of the whole world, was fully endured by the Saviour of the world."  Now these are not Scriptural words, nor words of the Church, and however they may be true *in a sense*, I should fear to argue from them against the obvious apparent meaning of Scripture, in such cases (e.g.) as that of David, and the others alleged in the Sermon.  Besides, (I am almost afraid to write it, but is it not so, that) this argument, literally taken, would exclude eternal as well as temporal punishment from those for whom He died ; and, therefore, with no few unhappy religionists of these days, we should be driven to deny either eternal punishment or universal redemption.

I should have thought that all we know is, " Christ's Sacrifice is in some way a satisfaction to God's justice for our sin," but *how*, we are not told.  Then with regard to those who seem to pass through life without temporal punishment for their faults, we surely know neither their faults nor what they may have to endure already ; much less do we know what Death and Judgment may be to them.

The Almighty has stores of chastening secret to us, as well as of mercy in its more placid form ; and I believe that those whom we have every reason to believe His most beloved, have always most earnestly welcomed those pains which they hoped, in some unsearchable way, might help to purify them.  This applies, I think, among other forms of suffering or penance, to that which Dr. Pusey (taking up our Lord's express warning) has dwelt on in a way which perplexes you. The shame of Confession is a most grievous penance, but is it not a necessary part of Repentance? and does it at all interfere with the completeness of pardon? The instances you allege of the faults of Saints do not appear to me to tell against this. Who knows how much they may have undergone from the consequences of their sins, or how earnestly they may have confessed them, and taken the shame upon themselves?

Then as to the difficulty of reconciling judgment according to works with a full and free pardon; since both are distinctly declared in Scripture we must believe both, though we could not at all reconcile them. But when we recollect the infinite degrees of reward, which He, we know, has in His Treasure House, we seem so far a little assisted in imagining how this may be.

I will not now enter into the explanation of the passage from S. Jerome, it may very well be overstrained, and yet the general doctrine be right. But even taken literally, it appears to me to follow quite as logically from such texts as S. Matt. xvi. 27, as the opposite kind of inference from the texts that speak of pardon. (By-the-bye, Ezek. xviii. 22, and such places, do not seem to exclude our confession, but the upbraiding of those who hear us, after pardon.)

On the whole, would not the idea of *Penance*

(surely a most Scriptural idea,) if we would accept and realize it, of itself supply a sufficiently practical answer to the kind of embarrassment which you (in common doubtless with many) feel? I do not mean Penance humanly inflicted, only or chiefly, but rather Divine Chastenings — "sinners accepting the punishment of their iniquity."

To your last difficulty I would say that God leaves us free to resist what He works in us, (see Isa. xxvi. 12, which seems to me to contain both parts of the doctrine of justification,) and therefore we are justly punished if we do resist. But who can speak or think with perfect accuracy on such a subject as the exact boundary of His promptings and our free-will? Do you know Bishop Butler's "Analogy?" If not, it may help you to read it, especially the parts about Punishment as a means of probation and purification.

## LETTER LXIV.

### To a Lady, on the Absence of Conscious Love and Devotion.

My dear ——,

I am much confirmed in my opinion, that your distress is, in a great measure, what may be called "morbid feeling," and that the way to deal with it is, not so much by direct opposition as by refusing to attend to it, and turning the mind another way.

This, therefore, with such authority as I have, I enjoin you to do to the best of your power, at least until I see you again. Pray against it beforehand, but do not brood over it when it comes. I have no doubt that, if another person were to come to you with the same kind of trouble in heart, you would say to him, " If you had no kind of love for God, you would not be troubled at your want of love for Him ;" and this at once makes an unspeakable difference between your case and such as was supposed in that Sermon. I say this (which I am sure is true) for the chance of its being useful, but you are not to go on thinking about it, but to turn away from the subject entirely, and let your self-examination for the present rather turn upon the government of your thoughts, ways, and tempers, towards your fellow-creatures. This, I trust, by the blessing of God, will be an effectual help to you in all respects. May that blessing be on you for ever, dear daughter, is the sincere prayer of

Your affec<sup>te</sup> friend,<br>J. KEBLE.

## LETTER LXV.

### To the Same, on the Same.

My dear Child in our Lord,

I am truly sorry for your distress : yet in substance I fear I can say little to help you that I have not said before. It is a trouble to be borne, this consciousness of being so dull and dry when you least wish to be so : only take care that you do not grow impatient, as though you were hardly used in its being allowed : neither be too minute in searching out the reason of it, only let it make you more and more watchful of your general conduct, especially against the infirmities of your temper. Take care that you do not ask angrily, " Must I continue to serve God in slavish fear ?" Of course you must, if it be His will. Is it not infinitely better than not serving Him at all ? Do not dwell upon this subject ; do not allow yourself to be worked up into any bitter feelings about it. Every morning, as earnestly as you can, commit yourself in prayer concerning it to our loving Saviour, and then dismiss it. Do not fret about it between whiles ; you cannot help being grieved at it when it occurs in private or public devotion, but then also dismiss it as well as you can at the end, by an earnest wish before God, which wish will be in His ears a prayer, that He would forgive you what in it may be due to any fault of your own, and enable you to mend it : and for the rest, that He would either relieve it, or enable you to bear it as He knows to be best for you, and especially pray against all bitterness.

For reading I do not think anything so likely to do good as "Meditations on the Life and Death of our Lord." Do you know Isaac Williams' books on that

K

subject? if you have not studied them, you might try them.

God be with you.

Y<sup>r</sup> affec<sup>te</sup> Father in X<sup>t</sup>,<br>
J. K.

. . . . I think you ought not to indulge the some-what morbid feeling which you express about our Lord's own words, but neither need you violently overbear it. There is danger lest under the guise of humility, (and not I daresay without a mixture of true humility in it,) it may have a touch of the old danger—ill temper (so to speak) towards God. Might you not draw up for yourself a very short prayer to be used some time every morning, for grace to derive comfort for that day from His own words?

## LETTER LXVI.

### To the Same.

MY DEAR CHILD,

I am grieved to the heart at your distress, and the more as I cannot help fearing that it may be greatly owing to insufficiency in one who ought to know better how to help you.

It seems to me so entirely a matter of dreamy morbid imagination, that I could sometimes wish myself a physician as my only chance of being able to deal with it. This plainly shews that praying for you is at least one thing which one is bound never to neglect, and I hope not to do so.

In the meantime, what if you were calmly to consider (and set down ?) what thoughts and ways have done you good in previous attacks of this sort, and what you would say to another person who should describe to you such feelings as his or her own ? May He, who only can, effectually relieve you.

Ever y$^{rs}$ affec$^{tly}$,

J. KEBLE.

## LETTER LXVII.

### To the Same.

MY DEAR CHILD,

I am truly sorry to hear of your distress continuing, but I must put it to your own conscience, whether there is not in it somewhat of self-tormenting and wilful peevishness; and whether, *so far*, the remedy is not, by God's mercy, in your own power. I must beg you to ask yourself whether you are really endeavouring to shake off the morbid feelings which haunt you, as sincerely as you would endeavour to cure a tooth-ache. You refer to some similar trials in times past. Perhaps it might be well if you would tell me what was Mr. ——'s course, which you seem to say prospered then. May God

bless and relieve you! and He surely will if you are
not wanting to yourself. In Him

I am ever y$^n$ most truly,

J. KEBLE.

# LETTER LXVIII.

## ON ABSTAINING FROM SACRAMENTAL AND USING SPIRITUAL COMMUNION.

MY DEAR CHILD,

I am inclined still to think that it will be better
for you to draw back from Holy Communion for
a short time—the next Sunday or two—by way of
a serious check and warning to yourself, and of a
kind of penitential sacrifice, which may be blessed,
please God, with a greater measure of grace to resist in future the first promptings of rebellious fretfulness at finding your spiritual life dry and uncomfortable. And for your support in this banishment,
you will do well to use, at least on the Communion
days, some form of Spiritual Communion. If you
cannot find one to suit you in your books, I will
try to find one for you. May God bless and cheer
you.

Always in Him,

Y$^r$ aff$^{te}$ Father and faithful Servant,

J. K.

# LETTER LXIX.

### To the Same.

My dear Child,

I am full of thoughts and good wishes about you, for indeed I have not been quite free from self-reproach ; . . . . and it is a relief to me to find that you are not made quite ill. I daresay you are in the right in going on with what you have begun, yet I think surely it would be very wrong in you and me not to have regard to your bodily weakness in the manner of doing it. . . . .

I think it would be a good thing if I were to stop you, and send you away when your feelings begin to turn the comfortable ordinance into unprofitable self-tormenting. If I were to do such a thing, it would not be at all as blaming you, but as a possible way of helping you to command yourself: may our Lord visit you night and morning, and keep far from you all snares of the enemy: may His holy angels wait around you to keep you in peace, and may His blessing be upon you for ever, through our Lord Jesus Christ.

The shame and pain you feel in confession is to be accepted as a Penance, not to be brooded over as a fresh sin. Be comforted. What if, while you are so cast down, the angels should be more than ever rejoicing over you ?

Y<sup>r</sup> affec<sup>te</sup> Father in X<sup>t</sup>,<br>J. K.

# LETTER LXX.

### AGAINST SEARCHING TOO CLOSELY INTO MOTIVES.

MY DEAR CHILD,

My entire conviction is that your anxiety about your *motive* for what you do in the way of penitence is carried too far. *He*, on purpose, for the most part hides that point from us ; so that few, if any, shall be able to say in what measure they are influenced by love, in what by fear, and shame, and indignation, and such inferior, yet legitimate motives. You, my child, must learn to bear this painful doubt, and to be thankful that He releases and keeps you from wilful sin *anyhow*. You must pray and strive for love, but not be violently grieved, nor angry with yourself, should you still feel as if the lower motives alone, or nearly alone, were yours. . . .

Do not allow yourself, if you can help it, to sit for many minutes, moody and dreaming. Your judgments, your conduct, your feelings towards others —*that* is where your minute watchfulness should be, *there* will be the proof of your grief being accepted as real contrition, much more than in any consciousness you may seem to have of it at the time.

Your loving Father in Christ,

J. K.

# LETTER LXXI.

## On Persevering without conscious Faith
### and Love.

Dear Child,

Certainly I do not *understand* you. There is but One who can do that entirely: but I feel tolerably certain that I have as accurate a notion as is usually given to one man concerning another: and I still say to you the same, " Patience, seek patience." Try still to be good and religious, and Faith will in His good time come after ; or rather the *sense* of Faith. For no doubt, in the sight of Him who sees all, the soul, which, feeling as if it could not believe, resolutely perseveres in trying to go on as if it did believe, that soul believes, with a faith more and more acceptable the longer it stands so sharp a trial.

This is the substance of the chapter you ask me about : very good for you if you will receive it : only do not set yourself against it, nor yet think the worse of yourself, if you find you cannot be comforted by it at present.

Your loving F. in Christ,
J. K.

## LETTER LXXII.

### To the Same.

MY DEAR CHILD,

. . . . I should, according to my judgment of the case, strongly recommend your going to the Holy Communion to-morrow : but let it be with as earnest resolution and prayers as you can make, that you will not again so give way to your feelings as to go on absenting yourself from Church and Communion, for want of sensible comfort in such duties. In a word, pray for Patience ; it is the first, last, and middle thing for you to ask. And pray that I may not be found altogether unworthy to help and comfort you : and believe me always, dear child in our Lord, in Him your affec^{te} Father,

J. K.

## LETTER LXXIII.

### On the Binding Nature of an Engagement of Marriage made by a Minor.

MY impression certainly has been all along, that an engagement made by a minor, and not sanctioned, rather I should say positively disallowed, by a parent, is altogether null and void, according to the Law concerning Oaths and Vows in Numbers xxx. I mean as to the formal and quasi-ritual effect of it :

there may of course be circumstances attending it which may make it more or less binding on the parties in a *moral* sense, as matter of generosity and honour, and doing as one would be done by.

It is plain that what is said about the greatness of the penalty for violating betrothal does not touch this, because in this way of taking it, it is as if no betrothal had occurred. In modern cases, which might seem to tell the other way, one must take into account, that betrothal, by the Canon Law amounts much more nearly to marriage, than it does by our law. And I suppose that in such matters the safest way is to take the law of one's own land as one's rule, except it be against the law of God. The Canons, which forbid a betrothed marrying another, take betrothal for something more than what we call engagement, for they refer expressly to a solemn benediction given by the Priest, as constituting the sacredness of it. There is a good deal in Bishop Taylor coming more or less near to the subject.

I should be very sorry to encourage people to take things too easily, but in this instance, especially since the person is such as I understand him to be, there seems no obligation either legal or moral. I trust the parties will advise with some one who can give a far more complete answer.

## LETTER LXXIV.

### To a Young Lady on Accepting an Offer of Marriage.

I AM slow in considering what to say, and how to say it. And now I am writing, I fear I shall but disappoint you ; for the question which you ask me to decide for you is really and truly one which can only be decided by yourself, and in effect must be so at last. You know what the marriage vow is ; you know the conditions and objects of marriage, as they are sufficiently set down in the Marriage Service ; you know whether you can pledge yourself to the fulfilment of those vows without doing violence to your conscience. If you distinctly feel that you cannot, surely you must decline it. I cannot believe that those who love you would 'go on urging you to it. You see I put it upon the state of your heart and affections, waiving the consideration of any supposed vow, and not going into the question, *how* your heart and affections came to be such as they are, one way or the other. I hope you will not think this unkind. I am sure it is the safest way for one called on, as I am, to speak on such imperfect and scanty knowledge, and it seems to me that it would sufficiently decide your course. You must not, ought not, to say, I will be this man's wedded wife, unless you feel in your heart that you

quite entirely mean to be so, and trust that you are
not sinning in so doing. It is your own responsibility, laid upon you doubtless for good. I do not
see how any opinion of any other person can relieve
you of it. But He who has laid it on you, doubt
it not, will enable you to bear it after His will.
He has guided and fed you all your life long unto
this day ; He will not forsake you in such a trying
moment. He will help you and others to bear the
suspense, if the answer of your heart be still doubtful ; or the pain and disappointment, if it be other
than they might wish.

## LETTER LXXV.

### To the Father of an Illegitimate Child.

Dear Sir,

I wish to say a few words to you on a very painful matter. . . . I fear it is impossible for you to deny
that you are the father of ——'s child, and I do
beseech you to consider what a heavy burden this
ought to be on your mind. You are not like an
ignorant person, brought up amongst unprincipled
people ; you cannot but know that, however lightly
the world may treat such sins as these, the Bible
speaks plainly, and says, they who do such things,
cannot inherit the kingdom of God ; and that these
are the very sinful lusts which you renounced in
your Baptism and Confirmation, so that now you

have, by indulging them, cast away the blessing of your Baptism, and ought not to have a moment's peace of mind until you have some good ground to believe that you are in God's sight a true penitent. S. Matt. vii. 7—10; S. Luke xi. 5—13; S. Matt. xviii. 1—14.

You ought not to be easy for this plain reason, that if you should die before such a change has taken place in you, you are sure to be lost for ever. You cannot deny this without contradicting a great many plain words of God. Then, besides the danger of your own soul, what a burthen it is to have to answer for the souls of others, unhappy partners in such sins; innocent, perhaps, until corrupted by you; or if they had gone wrong before, plunged by you into deeper wickedness.

Remember our Lord Himself says, "Whoso shall be the cause of sin to one of these little ones, it were better," &c. Think what it must be to meet them at the last day, and to feel that you are the cause of their ruin — the devil's agent to prepare them for his kingdom, and not only them, but all others whom such bad example tends to corrupt.

Now I do not at all suppose that you ever intended all this mischief; nor do I doubt that, as a good-natured young man, you are sorry for the present misery of this poor young woman; but the mischief you see is done: you were carried away by your passion in spite of good instruction; and however sorry you may be now, surely experience must have taught you to mistrust yourself for the future. Surely you must feel that if you do not now turn over a new leaf entirely, and seek God's pardon and help in a truer and better way than you have hitherto done, there is no chance, but you will go on from bad to worse : and what will the end be ? For the sake of your parents, and for your own sake, I beseech you to think on these things now : you know as well as I do that the time will soon come when you will wish you had thought on them. If, according to our Saviour's and the Church's direction, you make use of me or any other clergy-man to advise you in the difficult work of steady repentance, you are aware, of course, that any clergyman is bound to keep people's secrets so applying to him.

But, in any case, repentance after such things must be a long and painful business, and particularly it will be quite necessary to make up your mind not to care for the foolish laughter of those who make a mock at sin. . . . . Do let me have the comfort of knowing that you intend to repent in earnest.

# LETTER LXXVI.

### To a Lady, on Submission to the Rules of a Religious House.

My dear Child,

I hope my not writing sooner, though I cannot excuse it, may have served the purpose of clearing your mind, as it has driven you upon thinking for yourself, and you seem now to find that you could not conscientiously make the required promises *to anyone;* which is so far an improvement in your position, as it takes away the uncomfortable thought of some vague feeling of mistrust towards any persons in particular.

I should not myself have construed the rules, . . . . as enslaving consciences and taking off responsibility in the way you apprehend. And I should have thought that anything of that sort which you may have heard of (I am too well aware that there is a risk of it), comes not from the system itself, but from the abuse of it by persons more or less morbid in their views and feelings. But I will not argue this point with you, only I would beseech you to think very gently of those who, construing such rules differently, do not think it wrong to submit to or enforce them.

For yourself, my dear child, I can only hope that

circumstances may enable you to go on in this kind of free obedience and voluntary work in which you are now living. No one has a right to be angry with another because he is not able to receive counsels (if so be) of perfection, which at first he had been supposed able to receive. . . . I need not say to you that the more you feel obliged to decline binding yourself by written or spoken rules, the more should you endeavour to practise an unforced sweetness and self-denial in your behaviour to all; "free from all," you should so make yourself "servant to all." I feel very hopeful that, so doing, you will be enabled to be of great service both to the Sisterhood and to the penitents, with the cordial approbation of the Directors, and without any undue strain upon your own conscience and feelings.

I will not say more at present, hoping, as I do, to see you before long.

Y<sup>r</sup> affec<sup>te</sup> Father in Christ,<br>J. KEBLE.

## LETTER LXXVII.

### To the Same.

My dear Daughter in our Lord,

I really do not think that you need at all dread being committed further than you would think right by anything they propose to you: I mean com-

mitted beyond what is plainly on the surface of
the words.  And on the other hand, I hope and believe that they will make allowance for your being
unable in some respects to come up to the measure
of "hardness," which seems to them best for the
work.

Where all are so much in earnest, there must be
some way of going on comfortably together: but
one feels certain that there will always be more or
less of a call for patience and fair interpretations on
both sides.  Might it not be a good thing for you
to be on the watch for opportunities and little ways
of shewing confidence in them, and suiting yourself
to their wishes the more carefully in all indifferent
matters, because there *are* one or two things in which
you cannot exactly do so?  But this, and more,
I have no doubt you do.  Your account of yourself, which I have been just looking over (and which
renews my shame for not writing sooner), shews that
by His mercy you are in that way of conscientious
watchfulness, which is the straight way to have things
set right, and I daresay you watch your words particularly, and are careful not to let anything drop
which may say more than you mean (like what you
told me of) ; this care is more required in you than
in some others, because of a certain *point,* with which
you know how to express yourself, and which sometimes acts as a temptation to say what one afterwards regrets.

# LETTER LXXVIII.

## To the Same, on Changing her Confessor.

My dear Child,

Your kind notes from time to time have been a great and undeserved comfort to me, shewing, as I trust, that you find more and more that you are in the right place, and with the right persons, and that you and your work are getting more and more suited to each other. I know there are several points in your former letter which I ought to advert to; but I have not left myself time to do so now; and I do not like to keep you waiting for an answer to this morning's note. I wish, as I have often wished, that I were nearer at hand, to save you from any difficulties of the kind. The shrinking you feel is of course what all would feel in opening their grief to a fresh person, and it is clearly better, in the abstract, to keep to the same. Whether in this case this is overbalanced by the inconvenience of the journey, and by the incidental good effect of your shewing such unequivocal confidence in those near you, you can judge better than I. On the whole (unless it were thought best to transfer yourself to a Priest near at hand for the future), I should fancy it might be best for you to dispense with regular confession this time, with the full purpose (D.V.) of

L

supplying it when convenient. Any questions which had better be answered *vivâ voce,* you might ask of ——, telling only what would be necessary for them to answer, and this would shew confidence without the inconvenience of a change of Confessor. I hope to write again soon.

Always your loving Father,<br>J. KEBLE.

## LETTER LXXIX.

### AGAINST INDULGING IN SELF-REPROACH.

MY VERY DEAR CHILD,

Now that our Confirmation is over (and with many things about it to make one very thankful), I may write a line or two to you, of whom I am so often thinking; especially at 9 o'clock A.M., on those days (rare and far between) when I do as one ought at that hour. I cannot help imagining sometimes, that this visit may be almost too trying for your spirits: and among other fancies, I sometimes say to myself, I hope she does not give way to those thoughts of self-reproach which I know did at one time trouble her; as if this continued helplessness were a token of displeasure. Believe me, my dear daughter in Christ, such a feeling ought not to be encouraged, any further than as it may help to keep one humble and thankful at having so much more in the way of blessing than one could possibly deserve. For this

purpose it may be well that such misgivings should
now and then cross the mind with a shade of sadness:
but what I am anxious to say to you, is, (I daresay
it is not needed, yet I will say it,) that they ought
not to be dwelt upon, nor encouraged.  I should fear
in such case their becoming morbid and really wrong;
for if one got to be at all positive about the matter,
it would be presumptuously pronouncing on what
must be a secret of Providence: and it would damp
both one's own thankfulness and others' happiness.
Therefore I should say, when such an idea comes
across you (which from time to time I should think
it probably would), deal with it as you would with
the first stirrings of anger: you cannot help feeling
them, but your business is to put out the spark at
once.  When it has roused you it has done its work,
and so has this misgiving (supposing there *be* any
ground for it) when it has made itself felt *as* a misgiving.  Now whether there be any ground for it or
no, is perhaps a question not to be solved in this
life: certainly the mere fact of your delayed recovery does not at all tend to solve it, as you yourself would, I am sure, be one of the first to see and
urge in the case of another person.  Do not, then,
dearest child, I beseech you, take this trouble as
a token of anger, but rather as a token of more than
fatherly love from Him who, perhaps, knows, that
your lot in life would be too happy, your cup too
richly filled with blessings, which, however pure, are

yet of this earth, were it not for this drawback. Look
on it so, as coming from a Father, and do not seek
to measure exactly whether any of it, or how much,
is penal. The Church, you know, in the Visitation
Service, mentions two causes for which sickness is
sent unto men, but does not set us upon determining,
which is the cause in our own case, how much we
are concerned in the one and not in the other. In
the matter referred to, you did for the best at the
time : you did not wilfully do wrong : if there were
a mixture of human frailty in the motive, you patiently and lovingly submitted to your Father's way
of curing you. All this is good and healthy: let
this be the course of your thoughts, but do not
beyond this indulge in self-reproachings : if they
come, put them away. This is my earnest advice
to you ; very likely you may not need it, but you
will, I am sure, excuse me for offering it. I feel so
certain, that if the other line had been taken, equal
or sharper misgivings would have ensued : and as
far as one dare speculate, I see such great providential good arising out of what was done. May God
grant that you may be able to tell me you have
no heart-ache of the sort which I apprehend ; or at
any rate, that you are resolved by His grace, as
a matter of duty, not to indulge it. . . .

## LETTER LXXX.

### TO A FATHER, ON THE DEATH OF HIS SON.

WHAT can I say to you . . . to thank you as I ought for your most comfortable letter. I knew it would be full of comfort, but this somehow is beyond my expectation ; . . . it looks to me like a fresh world opened for you, both of sorrow and of consolation. Well do I know what thoughts I ought to have of it, so far as I am myself concerned ; but for you all, one's heart can rest in nothing but leaving you, as it were, to Him Whom you can all but see taking your child up in His arms, and giving him His final blessing. I hope not to forget what you speak of in my prayers, such as they are : I shall ask that for which I hope as confidently as I well can for any special mercy—that this merciful trial may be fully blessed, to all the purposes for which it is sent ; for correction, where need may be; for high and heavenly improvement to you all. May you have many a more joyful Christmas. I do not think you will ever have a much *happier* one in this world. Forgive me if I say what I ought not. I have been much interrupted in writing this. Your letter this morning met one from ——, with a similar account of his only boy. . . . This evening brings a much worse account than any before of ——. So

His people seem to be fast entering into their rest, or rather, His rest.

Ever your loving and grateful,

J. K.

## LETTER LXXXI.

### To the Same.

MY VERY DEAR FRIEND,

I must write you one line on this soothing and trying day—the most trying and soothing of all but one in the whole year (at least, I suppose it must be so to a parent)—to say that we are thinking of you, and have been so all day. It seems to make a *third* in our own troubles in a remarkable manner. ... One tries to feel it all, and is but the more convinced that there is but One who really can do so. May He bless your new year.

Ever believe me yours gratefully and lovingly,

J. K.

*H. V., Innocents' Day.*

## ·LETTER LXXXII.

### To the Same.

JUST one little word, my dear kind friends, to say how much we think of you all, and comfort ourselves with the assured hope how much you are thought of in Paradise, more and more, as your treasures are more abundantly gathered in there.

"Fast in Thy Paradise, where no flowers can wither,"

it seems to come naturally into one's mind when one thinks of dear ——, and her love of pure spring flowers continuing to the last. . . . . I do trust and hope that the remembrance of such may go on winning and purifying many, to whom God's Providence has made. them specially known, long after they have been taken out of our sight. It is a fragrance which, please God, can never pass away. To Him be all the praise. He will accept it, even from the unworthiest.

## LETTER LXXXIII.

To a Lady, on Temptations to Self-complacency, and on Imperfections in Self-examination and Contrition, and Incompleteness in Confession.

Very dear Child,

I have no doubt that what you complain of is perfectly correct, viz. that in your daily notes you do not put down the worst thing; that worst thing being, in fact, a sort of blind vein of self-satisfaction, which would fain accompany you all along in what you try to do for God, for your neighbour, and your own soul. I dare say this is your principal temptation, but you must still keep worrying it away by such considerations as you yourself allege to impress

yourself with its utter folly. You must pray especially against it (vide Ps. cxxxi.), you must do penance for it by trying inwardly to turn away from,
and be pained at the affectionate praise even of
those whom you would most wish to approve you.
You may, by God's grace, both accept the affection
with joy, and yet shrink with real dread from the
praise, and, as it were, stop your ears to it : e.g. anything of the sort uttered by certain revered friends
would naturally recur often to one's memory, and
one would be tempted to dwell on it ; then it would
be a real and good act of penance to turn from the
recollection and think of something else.

Again (I speak it in doubt, but you will judge
if there is anything in it), could you sometimes contrive for yourself little penances, in the way of dress,
or by otherwise doing violence to your taste, when
you are conscious that you have forgotten yourself
in the way of self-praise or of seeking praise ? Such
self-denials would, I apprehend, be as effectual in
the way of penance to you, as fasting, or watching,
or hard lodging, to those who can bear it. I am
not sure that you need trouble yourself at the mere
circumstance that you do not *feel* so much, after
a time, the downfalls, which at first made themselves
so keenly felt. It is the nature of emotions of all
kinds, good, bad, and indifferent, to be most felt,
when the object is new, or newly revived : but the
measure of your condition is not your feeling but

your practice : if the sins are more watched against, and occur more rarely, less flagrantly, and are of shorter continuance, it is an improvement much more to be trusted, and more indicative of real contrition, than if you felt them as bitterly, or more so, without that practical improvement. One would wish and pray for both marks ("Oh, that my head were waters," &c.), but the former state is more healthful and hopeful, generally. As to not having told all, one knows, of course, that you could not have done so, nor ever will be able to do so: but so it is with all penitents. He knows all before, yet forgives and heals them as in the Gospel to-day, and helps them, if it be needful, to tell all the truth the next time. As a general rule, do not worry yourself afterwards with musing how much better you might have done : only look calmly at your short-comings, with a view to amendment the next time. I hardly know how to frame your questions for self-examination, even if I more exactly remembered the points you mentioned to me when you were here. My memory, I fear, gets worse and worse. But I will try according to what your letter suggests, though I doubt not you are already in the way of asking yourself the same things. I dare say you inquire of your conscience, "Has there been, since the last self-examination, any marked instance of *self-praise*, such as to be at once recollected? or of seeking praise for its own sake? or of fretfulness at the change you speak of, or for any reason? (I mean fretfulness *indulged,* for one cannot help shadows crossing one's mind), or of ill-advised talk about others?"

Believe me, dear child, very affectionately your Father, in Him Whom we would serve,

J. K.

## LETTER LXXXIV.

### ON SPECIAL SUBJECTS OF SELF-EXAMINATION.

MY DEAR CHILD,

.... As far as I can judge from the samples you have sent me, I could imagine that it would be very useful in giving you method and courage, and a sense (D.V.) of getting on, and in hindering you from spending too much time and thought in self-reproachings, if you were to select some one out of the several subjects to which your memoranda refer, to be, for a time (so to speak), your special battle-field. That is, that for a time, say to the beginning of Lent, you should set yourself to overcome especially some one fault; and by way of naming one, which will be easily marked and felt, I would propose that it should be, what I see you repeatedly complain of, inconsiderate words or ways regarding ——. You might make this your special matter of watching and prayer and self-examination, and contrive little penances (I mean not violent, though real as far as they went) for any failures in it : and besides the direct advantage of curing the fault itself, it would be of much indirect help in other things. Of course, one may help oneself very much in such a case, by using oneself to think how soon the time may come when we shall long after such opportunities of dutifulness, and it will be too late. I will not give you any further rule at present. Your plan of setting down, and (if you think it better) sending to me but one out of many *specimens*, is a very good one, I think. I quite understand them to be only such. In the nature of the case they must be so to almost all people. You gladden my heart, dear child, by your sweet words about my other child (or grandchild?); I always thought the sunshine was *in rerum naturâ*, which would make her blossom out.

In Him your loving F.,
J. K.

## LETTER LXXXV.

### ON PENITENTIAL EXERCISES FOR LENT.

DEAR CHILD,

What you feel about Lent is, I imagine, what all, or almost all, feel, who set themselves to observe it in earnest ; even though they are ever so much guided: *how* to do it, or how they have done it, must be to them as unsatisfactory a question as

what to do can be to you.  Those who have been,
or yet in some sense are, under the dominion of
some known and wasting sin, have so far a more
definite course ; where, by God's mercy, that is not
the case, the perplexity you speak of, painful as
it is, may well be borne with true thankfulness,
that one's case is not far more miserable.  That
will be one way of improving it.  Another, of course,
is to make it an occasion of prayer, e.g. if you were
to turn the substance of your last letter to me into
an address to Him, pouring out yourself to Him at
large, stating to Him all the difficulties and cravings
which He knows already, but loves to be told of,
as Moses, Job, Jeremiah, David did.  The 143rd
Psalm, if I mistake not, is just in the key, to which
your heart will respond.  And among uninspired
writings there is a book on the list of the Christian Knowledge Society, " The Meditations of James
Bonnell, Esq.," in which spiritual troubles are dealt
with in a way, perhaps, to soothe and help you.
If you cast yourself before Him as well as you can
in this spirit, and tell Him all, and beg Him to
think for you of all that you know not how to
tell Him ; He will as surely help and guide you
as He has taught you to call Him Father.  You
will judge better than I whether it would not help
you to do all this in writing.  I would wish it to
be done quite at large, and not to take up any
very long time at once, so as either to excite or

weary you more than can be helped. I should
hope and expect that upon using this, or some such
devotional help, you would be guided in the choice
of times and forms of prayer, and exercises of self-
denial, as may best suit your case. Meanwhile, I
would propose one or two obvious things. 1. That
you should annex something Lenten—a collect, a
verse, or part of hymn—to each of your stated offices
of private devotion. 2. That you should, at some
time in the day, practise meditation, for at least
half-an-hour (and here again the pen might be useful), on some Lenten subject: e.g. on Monday on
Contrition: Tuesday, Confession; Wednesday, Penance (voluntary and involuntary); Thursday, Intercession; Friday, our Lord's Passion in some of its
details; Saturday, Resignation. The Sunday subject might be suggested by the Sunday services.
Direct self-examination *might*, and prayer of course
*ought*, to be always part of this exercise. Modes of
self-denial are more difficult to suggest. Sleeping on the ground is rather an extreme measure,
and I could not recommend it in your case, as far
as I can judge. It would either hurt your health,
or you would soon become used to it, and it would
make small difference. Two cases appear to me,
in which it *is* desirable—as penance or check to
grievous sin, or as inuring people to necessary privation in missionary labours: but these are not here
in point. *Dress*, I believe, I have mentioned before.

I suppose that in this respect ladies are not altogether free agents, otherwise one might fancy there
might be a good deal of room for self-denial, without
ostentation or singularity. You mention amusing
books and talk; perhaps the quantity of these, incidental to your position, might be lessened by a
little arrangement; and it seems to me that it
would be probably a real, and therefore an acceptable, sacrifice. Again, it is a good Lenten exercise
to refrain from speaking, when it would tend to
blame others, or get credit to oneself, unless it be
a matter of duty; and this alone will furnish a good
deal of matter for watching and self-examination.
Then there is forcing oneself to pay or prolong unpleasant visits to people of various ranks; to do
useful work, writing or study against the grain, and
other disagreeable things, which experience will suggest: and some of these which I have mentioned
may, perhaps, not inconveniently be appropriated to
some one day of the week, or otherwise practised
on something of a system.

Y<sup>r</sup> affec<sup>te</sup> F. in Him whom we serve,

J. K.

## LETTER LXXXVI.

### Giving Subjects for Meditation.

.... My notion is, that in the "Devotional Helps"
you have just what you asked of me for meditation.

But I will set down what occurs to me, endeavouring to combine the subject of the season in each case with the matters which you specify as troubling you. The subject of next week is the Light of God's Truth (Collect), shining in us before men (Epistle), even in trouble (Gospel). Think, then, with yourself, when you are dispirited about the matters temporal or spiritual which trouble you, on such places as (1.) Isa. l. 10, 11 ; (2.) when you forget your prayers or the like, on S. Luke xxiii. 45, 46 : (3.) when you cannot get over dislike to any one, on S. Matt. xxvi. 47—50 ; (4.) when it vexes you to be treated as bodily weak or ill, think of S. John xix. 28—30 ; (5.) when it is hard not to be with sick friends, &c., think of S. John xi. 3—6 ; (6.) when your soul refuses comfort, think of David (Ps. lxxvii.), and of Jacob (Gen. xlviii. 15, 16), and of our Lord (S. John xix. 27, 28) ; (7.) When you feel as if you had been hasty towards ——, think of her love as an image of God's, and how He loves and turns all to good (Isa. lxvi. 13). Try this for the present, and let me know how it works. I will not now assign you any further penance, but serve God, be cheerful, and do not lean too much on any of us. Beware of " Hero worship."

# LETTER LXXXVII.

### On Writing when out of reach of Personal Confession.

My dear Child, .

I think it a very good plan for you to write
down the main points you would wish to speak of,
if verbal confession were convenient; and whether
you send it to me or not, that you should lay it
before Him in prayer, and offer to Him solemnly
all your languor and short-comings to be healed
in His own good time and way. When you have
done this solemnly, first in your preparation, and
afterwards in Holy Communion itself (as you know
Thomas à Kempis did), then you will have a right
to say to whatever it is that keeps on disquieting
and disheartening you so about everything, "I have
put the matter into my Saviour's hands, and there,
by His grace, I will leave it." I speak this of all
vague and general impressions, e.g. that one never
loves enough, that what one does right one does
from the wrong motive, &c. Where any command-
ment is distinctly broken, let the breach be distinctly confessed with prayer, and, if need be, by
that confession repeated at stated times, but do not
worry yourself perpetually about it. Such a course

tends in a mind like yours to mere useless regret, or even fretfulness, which can do no one any good.

Y<sup>r</sup> loving Father in our Lord,

J. K.

## LETTER LXXXVIII.

To the Same.

Dear Child,

I quite agree with you that the most comfortable thing for dear ——, would be to have some one to whom she might entirely defer, and who would entirely sympathise with her; in a word, to have her father back again. But there is this token of its not being the *best* thing for her, that Providence has denied it, perhaps, in part, for this very purpose, that she may make her crown brighter by facing trustfully and enduring patiently the distress of her present position. . . . Your account of the kind of trouble to which she would probably be exposed by accepting the ministrations of the Parish Clergy, enables me to judge more clearly of the case, and perhaps I may have already met it in part by something which I said in my hurried note to her on Sunday ; viz. that my own custom, when I am not celebrating, is not to look at all to see how the service is conducted. For you know, my dear child, Who it is that really offers, and that it is His Church which ministers,—Christ the Priest, and His Church the

M

Deacon; and I think we ought to arm ourselves
with faith, that we shall not suffer nor lose any
part of the blessing by the ignorance, or error, or
even positive wickedness of the human instrument;
we should take it for granted, that the celebrating
Priest has the same intention as the Church. The
special point which you mention, the neglect to observe the Rubric with regard to the " Remains," is
easily obviated in private Communion, because care
can be taken to have some one with the sick, who
will deal with it reverentially, even if the sick person
himself be too helpless.

I have heard that the Clergyman of —— is one
who would sympathize. But the Curate himself
would be far best. You will judge how much or how
little of this to mention to him or to anyone.

Y<sup>r</sup> ever affec<sup>te</sup>,

J. K.

## LETTER LXXXIX.

ON IDLE THOUGHTS; AND ON FAMILIAR INTERCESSIONS.

MY DEAR DAUGHTER IN CHRIST,

Your letter has been a great comfort to me, for
I never know at the time whether I am not doing
more harm than good.

With respect to the distress of idle chimerical
thoughts,—in which I can greatly sympathize, having

had in very old times just the same doubt of the reality of things which you describe,—might it be worth while to try the effect of short Ejaculatory Prayers, or of forcing oneself to contemplate (if within reach) a picture of our Lord crucified, or some other such memorial of some of the great and ever-present realities? For such a state of mind is like a real dream, out of which one needs to be effectually startled.

I think that you need not scruple applying to persons in your intercessions, any name or title which you would deem consistent with respect to call them by, in speaking of or to them. You know they would be sorry to be left out of your prayers through any scruple of that kind.

I will endeavour to put into this cover the little night service which I think I spoke of to you. *Pray* have· no scruple in writing and mentioning things to me, and believe me always,

Very affectionately yours,

In Him whom we would serve,

J. KEBLE.

# LETTER XC.

To the Same: In Worship our Lord's two Natures
not to be Separated.—Suggestions as to Dealing
with Faults; and for Lent.

My dear Child in Him whom we hope to Serve,

I am almost inclined to think that it may be as
well for you not to analyse your motives and feelings
in such a matter as your letter chiefly refers to. It
is enough that the particular mode of helping thought
does not suit you; that it causes perplexing thoughts
about our Lord's two Natures. I should say, by all
means let it alone, and employ the simple Cross,
or whatever help you find more available.

It may be well as a general rule, to add, that it
never has been the way of Christian Devotion to
distinguish *in Worship* between our Lord's two Natures. We worship His Person Who is both God
and Man, without scruples or ideal separations : but
we do not call upon His Saints or Angels, because
He has not commanded us to do so.

This is to my mind the simple, true, and sufficient
account of the difference in that respect between
the reformed and unreformed Church. I should be
loth to charge the latter with confusion in its doctrine of our Lord's two Natures, in consequence of
its receiving these Invocations : although I much

fear that some such evil consequence is too likely to flow from it, especially just now.

You speak of ill consequences from even so much seclusion as you are now living in: might not that seclusion be modified so far as is necessary, by intercourse with some of the ladies who are working there as you are, and with whom you must have more or less of sympathy? If your present rules forbid this, might I with propriety write to ——, to propose some modification?

I believe that the "Aids" recommends a person to attack one fault at a time; and where the faults are distinctly perceived, I suppose it would be the most practical way.

About a rule for Lent, I think I should connect it with this last subject; i.e. might it be well to choose as a subject of Morning meditation, and afternoon or evening prayer, some one of the faults which one wished to correct, or of the virtues which one wished to acquire? If you approve of this, and will mention any subject, I can suggest such devotions as occur to me.

About confessing again, you must judge for yourself. Advice may of course be written, but Absolution must be given in person. We can easily manage it if you wish. I am, dear daughter in our Lord, affectionately yours,

J. KEBLE.

# LETTER XCI.

### ON PREPARATION FOR HOLY COMMUNION.—
### ACTS OF PENANCE.

##### MY DEAR CHILD FOR OUR MASTER'S SAKE,

. . . . I quite understand the difficulty of suiting our common books, such as "Steps to the Altar," to the use of very frequent Communicants: but, to my shame be it spoken, I am very unready with any plan for meeting it. The only thing that comes into my head is to suggest the use of the " Aids to a Holy Life," for the additional Communions, keeping the "Steps to the Altar" for the first Communion (say) in every month, and then using general confession. For the Thursday, one might take particular confession, according to Mr. Bund's rules, of the special fault which one is most engaged in warring against. For the three other Sundays, any three of his general heads which one felt most occasion to attend to—for each Sunday, one.

Or one might take the four first sentences of the Offertory, which always appear to me as if they were selected with a view to Self-examination ; the first, as against vainglory ; the second, against worldly-mindedness; the third, against selfishness : the fourth, against hypocrisy. One or other of these might well furnish matter for trying and judging oneself for half-a-week. In short, there is ample material in the book I mentioned, but devotions are wanting, and you would have to select them for yourself.

If the notion, thus generally stated, seems to you likely to be useful, you will soon, I think, find suitable prayers and Psalms and texts: and I shall be glad to mention for your consideration any which occur to me.

With regard to the special obligations and trials of a Sisterhood, I regret to say that I am really quite ignorant. I may imagine and infer about them, but I cannot say I know. But if you cultivate right tempers according to such rules as are given in the little book which I have mentioned, I cannot think that you will be practically at a loss, in the duties either of that, or any other state of life, to which you are fairly called.

About acts of Penance, I hardly know what to say. You know yourself what your little tastes are, and inclinations in indifferent matters: bearing these in mind, and at the same time watching your inclinations to wrong, you will be taught the way to correct the latter by the former.

My dear Child, God bless you.

Yours always affec<sup>lly</sup>,

J. K.

# LETTER XCII.

### ON DISTRACTIONS.

MY DEAR CHILD,

I do not wonder that the increased quantity of work and responsibility, especially with the sore trial of the withdrawal of Mr. ——'s aid, proves so bewildering, and such an interruption to your devotions. It is but natural that it should be so : it is as when I am near the schoolboys in church, and am drawn aside to notice their behaviour. You have a large family to think of, and it is impossible that this should not be continually interfering with your attention in times of devotion.

But do not let this confound or alarm you. Use yourself, in the course of the work itself, to say in your heart short ejaculations now and then, so offering your work to God as it goes on ; and do not allow yourself to brood over the imperfection you may be conscious of in what you have been doing ; offer it all up, with all its blemishes, as a sacrifice in Christ's name. Turn your troublesome thoughts themselves into prayers, you will find them fitting on, oftener than you might expect, to the regular prayers of the time or occasion. *Every* thing, we know, fits on to the Lord's Prayer.

I do not recommend any great change in the

number and order of your devotional services, they should rather be frequent than long, and I would not be disheartened, nor tempted *voluntarily* to omit any of them (business I dare say will often compel omissions) on account of the difficulty of attending, or the like. Prayer, which seems to yourself cold and formal, offered and persevered in as a duty, may win you a greater blessing than that which seems to flow most freely, and which gives most comfort at the time. What a comfort there is in considering Who said, " The spirit is willing, but the flesh is weak." .... I do not suppose that if we met I could in substance give other advice than what I have now written, which, indeed, comes to little more than "go on in cheerfulness and patience."

I think you will find that by His mercy, before long, your prayers and work help one another : but whether you feel it or no, I have no doubt that they do. God bless you, my dear daughter in Christ, and restore, if it be His will, our dear sick friend.

In Him your affectionate Father and Friend,

J. KEBLE.

## LETTER XCIII.

### ON THE SAME.

.... I BEG of you not to be too much distressed if you find no great difference, for ever so long a time,

in respect of the wanderings which harass you.   Do
your best in reason against them, and then bear
them as a trouble, rather than accuse them as a fault.


# LETTER XCIV.

## On Wishing for Death.

My dear Child,

Your letter both grieves and refreshes me.   May
He, who can, give you and all of us, the full consolation of the refreshing part of it, without as yet
realizing the part which grieves one.   You will not
think it unkind if one still prays that you may be
spared and helped to do more and more work for
Him.   But He knows best; as He willeth, so be it.
. . . . Who that believes and *realizes*, can help desiring to depart and to be with Christ? but like
all other desires, which we cannot help, it should be
with humility and submission, and fear of presumption, and charitable care for others.


# LETTER XCV.

## On Obedience to one's Confessor.

My dear Child,

In reply to your friend's question.   "To obey a
person as one's Confessor," might mean differently
in the mouths of different people : but, I suppose

in this instance, it means absolute unquestioning obedience in all instances, and that, as it should seem, to a comparative stranger. I could not myself make such a demand, unless, from previous knowledge of the case, I was tolerably sure it was necessary, e.g. to prevent a Romanizing conscience from trifling with me, and with the ordinance.

And if the promise ought not to be demanded, it cannot, I imagine, be wrong to decline making it. Only one should be very careful not to be guided in the matter by prejudice or self-will. I wish the former adviser may recover sufficiently to be consulted : his opinion would be worth a hundred given at a distance.

Farewell, my dear friend and daughter in Christ, and believe me always,

Affectionately yours,<br>J. KEBLE.

## LETTER XCVI.

### TO AN UNDERGRADUATE.

Do not be downhearted ; your difficulties are sure to occur to an earnest youth at this time, and your safe way will be, to go on as you have begun, keeping to the Prayer-book as nearly as you can, and without any special profession, or marked and singular observances; letting people find out, if so it happens, that such is your rule.

If you can get hold of a sermon in Newman's first volume on S. Matthew v. 15, it will shew what I mean.

Whatever people do, or decline to do, as to confession, 1. should not go upon *feeling*, one way or the other, but upon calm consideration, with prayer.

2. Should not be allowed to lessen their sense of their own responsibility.

3. To whomsoever the confession is to be made outwardly, it should be made distinctly to our Lord beforehand, in the conviction that He knows it all beforehand, and has declared His will that it shall be *somehow* made known. S. Luke xii. 2.

This I write, not to bias your judgment, but worth serious thought in any case.

Ever yours most lovingly,

J. K.


# LETTER XCVII.

## To THE SAME.

I MUST begin, as I said, to write you a few lines when I can; and, first of all, though I daresay it is not necessary to remind you of it, your difficulties about which you have written, being all about outward profession, and how to let your light shine before men, one may hope that, by the blessing of God, your heart and conscience are right, so that as you are sworn, so you are stedfastly purposed to keep *all* His righteous judgments ; not so much to consider whether what He commands or forbids seem great or small, but simply that He *does* command or forbid it, and to examine yourself daily and order your ways accordingly.

Having thus (humanly speaking) a clear conscience in matters that are known only to God and yourself, you may, with less fear of self-deceit, apply yourself to others, and plan how to do most good to them.

And as this latter is, of course, a subject of special prayer, so that prayer, to be effectual, requires constant watching, not to incline to wickedness in one's own heart. Zeal, even self-denying zeal for the Church, may do good to others, and yet prove a dangerous delusion to a man's self. This is the foundation. I daresay I need not have said anything about it. Now this being pre-supposed, and what I said in my former letter about obedience to the Prayer-book added to it, here is at once a real and continuing witness borne to Christ ; all the more telling, because it is silent and unobtrusive, felt, rather than observed, by others ; and the less conscious you are of it yourself, as to its effect on others, the better. Indeed, I suppose it would be a good prayer to God, to hide from us any good that we are allowed to do, except so far as may be necessary for one's guidance and perseverance.

Well, a young person going on thus, meets, of

course, with well-meaning persons, who propose to him, or set him an example, how to do good, or witness for Christ in some special way. He thinks of it in his prayers, he turns it over in his mind, he sees clearly, perhaps, that even if he demur to the thing itself, the principle of it is good, and good to be brought to his thoughts, reminding him, perhaps, of some point of duty or devotion, which it will be well for him to think more of than he has done, e.g. in the union for prayer; if a man saw reason, or if his parents, &c., were in the mind to doubt, yet the substantial point is secured by his promising to say the Lord's Prayer, or the petition in the Litany, or the Collect for all conditions of men, in that special sense, so often.

But on all matters, especially where there is anything demonstrative or unusual, there is nothing like a good and willing adviser at hand, and such you will find Mr. ——. If you would like to speak to him, but feel shy, I will ask him to speak to you, and you need not fear to be as unreserved with him as you may find comfortable. I don't say at once, Take him for a kind of director—for on *that* you would of course, in any case, consult your Father.

This is all I have to say now, except God bless you, and help you to act on the true meaning of S. Mark x. 21, and to go on serving Him cheerfully.

Your most loving,

J. K.

# LETTER XCVIII.

## To an Aged Clergyman under Spiritual Depression[1].

My dear Sir,

I learn from your nephew that you have sometimes expressed a wish to see me : I hope not to forget this, in case our lives should be spared, and anything bring me into your neighbourhood ; for indeed I should rejoice if I were permitted to be of any use or comfort to you, not only from the re-

[1] The following particulars, extracted from the letter to the Editor which accompanied Mr. Keble's, are inserted by kind permission of the writer. They give additional interest to the letter, witnessing as they do to the value of his words of Christian comfort and encouragement.

"My relative was dying at an advanced age, though with unimpaired faculties ; his body gradually wearing out without any pain or disease : but he was oppressed with a deep sense of his sinfulness, and fear that he had not been forgiven, and consequent absence of all comfort in prayer. One day, in answer to a suggestion to consult some others, the words burst from him, 'Oh that John Keble were here.' Though senior to Keble he had known him in early life. I at once, though a stranger to Keble, wrote to him, describing as well as I could the state of mind, and begged him to be kind enough to write. It drew from him the letter, of which I enclose a copy. As it may give to others the same comfort that it did to him, and be the means of smoothing the death-beds of others as it did his, I will not withhold it.

"Some days after its receipt he looked up to me suddenly and said, 'I am quite happy now,' and in the same quiet happiness of faith he died."

membrance of times past, when we used occasionally
to meet, and of mutual and dear friends now, most
of them, taken out of our sight, but (you will allow
me to say it) from a real debt of gratitude which
I owe you for having been, I believe, the first to draw
my mind towards the right way (so far as I have
attained to it) of dealing with "the little ones" of
the flock.   As I am not able to wait upon you,
I avail myself of a hint from your nephew, that
a few words in writing might be not unacceptable.

You feel, my dear Sir, (you would not wish to feel
otherwise,) what a nothing, and worse than nothing, is
what you have done for our Lord, compared with what
it ought to have been ; and the thought will at times
occur—"how is it possible that such an one can be
accepted ?" and the comfort and hope which you
know to be intended for all, seems somehow to be
denied to you, for the time.   Yet, at the bottom of
your heart, I am quite sure you do not doubt the
"comfortable words," especially that most comfortable word "all," with which we are so continually
encouraged.   The invitation is to "*all* that travail,"
it is "worthy of *all* to be received," it is for "*all*
that believe in Him ;" for *any* man that hath sinned
He is the Propitiation, and He is willing to be an
"Advocate."   I have no doubt you try to teach
this to yourself, as you have so often taught it to
others ; but you cannot always bring it home to
yourself ; you cannot always *feel* it true ; and this

alarms and perplexes you, as it has, and does, and will, thousands before, around, and after you. May I mention one or two methods of dealing with this trial, which, by God's blessing, may be useful to you —one or other of them?

I could say, for one thing, *make your account beforehand with this trouble coming upon you, as you would with a fit of bodily pain,* to which you might know yourself liable; and offer it to God as you would the bodily pain, in deep resignation, giving yourself up to Him, to deal with you, in this respect also, as He knows best. And, as we know that in some mysterious way, our bodily sufferings are united (if we take them rightly) to those of our Lord on the Cross, so we may venture to associate these sadder misgivings of the soul with the deep agony and sense of desertion which He vouchsafed to endure for us. And we may believe that, in ways known to Him, they are made instrumental to our final purification and salvation. One way in which this may happen, we may well believe, is this : the more entirely we are made to feel the worthlessness of all that we have ourselves been or done, the more are we thrown, wholly and solely, upon the merits of Him, who is our only Hope : and this deep and bitter feeling may be our Lord's providential way of causing you to cast all your care upon Him, as you no doubt endeavour to do, but feel that you do it but inadequately : this distress may render you more earnest in doing so; and "if there be first a willing mind"—you know the rest, and how fully it applies to the inward offering of Faith and Repentance, as well as to the outward one of Alms.  Once more; I should wish to say, I am continually saying, in effect, to persons in such trouble as you sometimes feel, "which do you really want of the Almighty? *Comfort* now, or pardon and acceptance hereafter?" The latter, of course: and it may be that the imperfection you complain of in the former, may greatly help towards that better thing; for " the Peace of God passeth all understanding."  Many, having it, feel as if they had it not : but many, alas ! wanting it, feel (like the Pharisees) as if they certainly had it.  Which is better : to kindle a fire of one's own, and compass oneself about with sparks, and have to walk in *that* light; or to walk in darkness, and have no light, only trusting (i.e. unweariedly trying to trust) in the Name of the Lord, and " staying yourself" as you may " on our God?"

Let me beseech you, dear Sir, to go on *trying* this ; and in a short time you will see and know what a Rock you have been indeed standing on.  Those who have gone on trying in earnest to love and to cling to Him, in spite of all discouragement, inward and outward, in spite of low spirits, and the bitter sense of uselessness and unworthiness, they of all others may be said to walk by Faith, not by Sight. How can they fail to receive the blessing of Faith ?

My dear Sir, excuse my running on in this way: sometimes the merest truism put in the homeliest way may help, where a higher sort of teaching has failed or might fail. But I trust that you will have more and more of that inward comfort and teaching which makes the soul happily independent of human suggestions, however well meant.

May the Almighty Guardian of our souls bring us all to Himself, when and how He knoweth best.

Pray, my dear Sir, for

Your faithful and affectionate Servant in Christ,

JOHN KEBLE.

## LETTER XCIX.

### To a Clergyman, who had written on behalf of Another in Doubt.

REV. AND DEAR SIR,

Your account, though sad, gives me much hope that this poor young lady, for whom it is impossible from your account not to feel very deep interest, will before long, by God's blessing, be restored to hope and comfort. There is no doubt that she gives way to feelings which do not at all belong to her case, because, as I have pointed out in a note on the very page you refer to, "hopeless misery," as far as we can judge from Scripture, can only be when this world is over. As long as a man lives, the word is spoken to him, "Come unto Me," &c. The question is then, If this lady heard that voice from Heaven, and knew that it was addressed to her, (which she could not doubt, since it says expressly, "All ye"), what would she do? which way would she turn? Let her do the same now, to the best of her power; and as God is true, she will find relief *sooner or later*, and continuing to do so, will find salvation at last.

I believe that in this I am uttering the sentiment of one of the wisest and best of human comforters, Thomas à Kempis, "Imitation of Christ," i. 25, n. 2. "When one that was *ᵉ*," &c. Perhaps if you can get this lady to put her mind to this thought, she may, by God's blessing, find in it what may help her.

I am away from home, but hope to be there after next week. Of course I would wish, if I could, to be spared just now any call to a distance. But if it seem that an interview is very desirable, and the lady cannot come to me, and wishes it, I will gladly wait upon her, when and where it may be

---

ᵉ [In the letter the passage is only referred to. It is as follows.—
EDITOR] :—

"When one that was in anxiety of mind, often wavering between fear and hope, did once, being oppressed with grief, humbly prostrate himself in a church before the altar in prayer, and said within himself, 'O if I knew that I should yet persevere!' he presently heard within him an answer from God, which said, 'If thou didst know it, what wouldst thou do? Do now what thou wouldst do then, and thou shalt be secure.' And being herewith comforted and strengthened, he committed himself wholly to the will of God, and his anxious wavering ceased."

most convenient. May God bless her, and you for
your charity towards her.

Believe me,

Truly yours,

J. K.

## LETTER C.

### ON THE SPIRITUAL TRIALS OF WEAK HEALTH.

MY DEAR CHILD,

Your trial is indeed a severe one, but by no means
unusual in various degrees among those whom God
calls to serve Him. It is indeed but one of those
belonging to sickness, and in that way you must
treat it, as when the doctor tells you you must not
go to Church. Its being inward instead of outward
makes no difference in this respect. To reconcile
you the more to this, suppose you regard it in this
light—that our Lord Himself is the Physician, and
your feeling that emotions exhaust you, is a token
from Him that He would not have you indulge in
them, but rather reserve yourself for any emergency
which His Providence may have in store for you,
and in which He may unmistakeably call upon you
not to spare yourself. Would it be well to consider
of some plan involving regular thought, which might
be profitable to yourself, and perhaps others, without involving emotion or any strain upon the feelings?
Could a series of subjects for thought on Sacred

History be contrived, which would in a certain
sense engage, without wearying or exciting you?
Could you find some friend near, or afar off, who
might take part with you in the same work, and
with whom you might interchange ideas and impressions; e.g. you could take a portion of Holy
Scripture, and deal with it as P. Young has set us
an example, not aiming to excite your own or others
feelings, but simply trying to set down the Truth
to His honour and glory. A very few days, and
a very short verse or two each day, would be sufficient for an experiment of this sort: and when you
had found out how to *tone* down your meditation
sufficiently, you might, perhaps, venture on longer
spells of it, and it might, by His blessing, come to
be something like soothing music, quieting and refreshing both body and soul. Do you remember
Wordsworth's poem on the Nightingale and the
Stock Dove? Depend on it, dear child, that the
languor which is brought on, not by sin or negli-
gence, but by the Visitation of God's providence,
will never tell against you in His account. Say to
yourself what you would to any one else, "He will
lay no more on you, than He will make you able
to bear." . . . However, I would recommend your
trying for the present something like what I have
suggested, if indeed I have made myself intelligible;
if not, give me a line, and I will try to explain, by
example or otherwise.

If it is not too exciting for you, I would recommend your practising Spiritual Communion, so as to supply, as far as may be, the want of more frequent actual Communion. Of the frequency you would soon be able to judge for yourself. But very likely you have already some rule of the kind.

Ever believe me,

My dear Child,

Your faithful friend in Him whom we would serve,

J. K.

## LETTER CI.

Spiritual Communion : Light in which to be Regarded.—Comforts under Spiritual Privations.

My dear Child,

I have been to Scotland again, and otherwise so hurried, that I have behaved very ill to you. Much do I fear that I have put you to a real Penance in so keeping you without an answer : and yet, in one respect, I should not be much surprised if my doing so turned out rather for your help. For I am sure that part of your trial is a temptation to lean too much upon direction, and to seek it too minutely in everything. So far I am not sorry that you have been thrown upon yourself, though ashamed that it should have been owing to my slothfulness. I think I must still give you the same general advice, to

meditate, with or without writing, either on the subjects I suggested, or (which I shall rather like at
this time especially) on any other course which may
present itself to your mind. . . . You might do this,
if you thought well, during this blessed week which
is coming.

Of course Spiritual Communion cannot be like
real Sacramental Communion, though none can tell
how great a blessing may attend it, properly used :
and it has no *promise*, that I know of, to distinguish
it from other Prayers : but the Church recommends
it ; Bp. Wilson and, I believe, Bp. Taylor and the *Paradisus Animæ*, exemplify it. I should think it might
be considered as in a certain way united to one's
latest Communion, as a continuation of the Devotions then offered, and so peculiar comfort and help
may very well be hoped for from it. Or you may
connect it prospectively, with your intended *next*
Communion, as part of your preparation.

And be sure, my dear child, that you have no
need to *indulge* perpetual fears and misgivings. You
have not to do with a hard Master, but with a loving
Saviour, who knows what you can bear, and lays
His burden upon you accordingly. It is His will
to try you by these spiritual privations, and by the
painful achings of heart which accompany them.
Try to make this His will yours, by patient submission to this trouble, so long as He allows it
to continue. Yet do what you can to allay it, by

prayer, by cheerful thoughts of His thousand great mercies every hour and minute multiplied upon you, by making your spiritual exercises rather frequent than long, and by turning your thoughts sometimes to intercession for others, in a large and detailed way, when self-examination and prayer for yourself seems (as it sometimes must) weary and unprofitable. I have been for two weeks at several times among the Forbeses, with whom you would have much sympathy. They are quite a large party in Edinburgh, and it is beautiful to see how they all light up the moment their kinsman the Bishop comes in sight. We are most thankful for the result of that trial. You should have seen the note that came from Ch. Ch. in reply to the Telegram conveying the news of it.

Ever, my dear Child,
Your Fatherly friend in our Lord,
J. K.

## LETTER CII.

### On Depressing Thoughts and Feelings, with allusion to his Sister Elisabeth.

My dear Child,

Among other thoughts, which come into one's mind at such times as we have been lately going through, and in which, in a certain sense (if it please God), I should desire to continue all my life—is a feeling how unkind and unsympathetic, without intending it, one must have partly been, and partly appeared, from time to time, in such troubles as yours, and especially in neglecting you so long as I have done. God forgive me: and I hope you will. I am sure I have never forgotten you for a day. But from what I hear of your health I fear you must have needed much comfort, and perhaps I might have given you a little. One thing I will mention to you—that when I think of my dearest sister in the depressing moments of her illness, I am, more or less, reminded of your troubles, for all her longing seemed to be for guidance—a feeling that there was some-thing to be done, and she did not know what— "would somebody be so good as tell her;" and her favourite verse next to the fifty-first Psalm, (which she continually recurred to) was "Teach me to do the thing that pleaseth Thee," &c. So, my dear Child, be so far comforted as that your trials in the way of bewilderment and seeming helpless-ness are so far like hers. For I quite think, that for all she seemed so calm, she had often to bear up against the same kind of feelings, in her time of comparative health. I fancy she found great help in writing out prayers and texts, and meditations (as I believe Bp. Wilson did). It seemed, I suppose, to throw them more entirely out of themselves, than when they were, as it were, composing for themselves ; I don't know whether this may suggest any thing to you. But if it does not suit, never mind.

My dear wife (D. G.) bore up well through the nursing. She never tried to sit up, and for the last ten days, or more, our sister from —— was with her, and my brother too, and they are still here. But C.'s breath is very distressing, though I believe Mr. —— does not think it alarming, and if the weather permit, we start to-morrow for Devonshire —Dawlish for the next week. Our kind, very kind love to you, dear Child, and to ——. Don't trouble to answer this but at your leisure.

Your loving Father in Christ,
J. K.

## LETTER CIII.

### MEDITATIONS—EXAMPLES OF.

DEAR CHILD,

After my manner I am answering your letter just too late, I fear, to be of any use. But really I am not sure that it would not be kinder to leave you to make your meditations for yourself. At least, this ought to be your *aim*, "to try to swim without corks" if you can, not in self-reliance, but in humble hope, that He who has given you a mind to try will help you also to what will please Him. (Another sad gap in my writing — we are got to Monday Evening!)

I will at once see what I can think of, though even now, I fear, I shall be too late for this post.

For what remains of this week I should like you
to meditate on the tokens of God's love in that third
chapter of Genesis ; how it kept more than even pace
with our sins, coming early in the morning, calling
us when we hid ourselves, inviting us to confess,
tempering each sentence with mercy, providing gar-
ments, withholding the fruit, which might have led
to a miserable eternity, &c.   And you may go over
whatever you can remember of His Providence towards yourself or others, which strikes you as being
in point.   Do the same next week with the History
of the Flood, and the week after with that of Abraham, and so on through Lent ; the Lessons of that
season being throughout, a wonderful exhibition of
God's Providence towards the chosen people, not
hard to apply to individual Christians.

Now I must thank you dear—with a great deal
of my heart for your kind help as to ——, which
I think will just help us to what we want.   It was
too bad to neglect you, whilst you were working so
hard for us.

Nevertheless believe me,

Y<sup>n</sup> ever lovingly,

J. K.

TWENTY-FOURTH SUNDAY AFTER TRINITY.

Christ's touch (Gospel) absolving His people from
their offences (Collect) and giving them joy and
strength (Epistle).

Think first, that even Christ's touch is not always a perfect cure at once. S. Mark viii. 22—25.

2. That the token of amendment is not always the *feeling* oneself better, but the *rising* to do God's work. S. Mark ix. 26, 27.

3. That the Holy Church *throughout all the world* is praying for you as in the Epistle, v. 11.

### TWENTY-FIFTH SUNDAY AFTER TRINITY.

A. The Lord our Righteousness (Epistle) ; B. leaving stores in His Church for us (Gospel) ; C. that we might plenteously bring forth good works (Collect). A. what troubles you ? (*a.*) past sin, (*β.*) abiding sinful infirmity. He is our righteousness in respect of both ; (*a.*) by His Cross, (*β.*) by His Spirit, trust Him and rejoice.

B. He has left His tokens, (*a.*) of pardon, (*β.*) of grace, in both the Sacraments and in Absolution. Think of Him as in person in all these.

C. Plenteously, i.e. constantly, (*a.*) not waiting, but doing the duty, be it little or great, of each minute as it comes, i.e. trying and praying to do so : (*β.*) not wishing fretfully for other circumstances, but forcing my will to be His. A miracle—but earnest Prayer will work it.

# LETTER CIV.

### FORGIVENESS NOT DETERMINED BY OUR FEELINGS.

MY DEAR CHILD,

I do hope we shall meet at —— this May or June, if not in April; but I take pleasure in believing that He helps you along, and keeps you out of any great perplexity or distress. Do not allow yourself to doubt of our loving Lord's forgiveness, when He tells you of it, as He distinctly does, both in Daily Service and in Holy Communion, you trying to come sincerely. Yet I had rather you felt as you do, than be so very happy as some are, if that happiness arises from their leaving the last accounts out of sight. Is not the truly filial feeling to accept the punishment of one's iniquity, praying that it may be in time, not in Eternity?—a prayer, which will surely be granted, if one is sincere in trying to repent. And you know the assurances of forgiveness: love is so far from being inconsistent with a state of penance, that it is rather implied in it.

Certainly that Oxford Cause is a matter for the prayer of all good Christians: and I do not know, humanly speaking, that we have much more than that to rely upon, but it will be something to bring out the fact, that as far as Judges and Courts go there is no help. If parents and guardians would do their duty in refusing to let their children be taught by him, the evil would cure itself in great measure.

Your loving Father in Him whom we would serve,

J. K.

## LETTER CV.

### THOUGHTS OF UNBELIEF IN OTHERS NOT TO DISTURB OUR DEVOTIONS.

MY VERY DEAR CHILD,

Your trouble about Celebration is very natural, but you are right in being a little jealous of its interfering with things more in your own power.

Such things as you have given me a sample of, had (as you say) better be set down *at the time*, ever so briefly, and you can send them to me or not, as you think it worth while.

Trouble yourself as little as you can about the unbelief of others, except to pray for them, the rather, as you know, at least of many, that in their unconscious hearts they really believe a great deal more than they seem to do, or are distinctly aware of themselves. Where should we be, if we let our devotions be interrupted, here because people are imperfect in the doctrine of the Sacraments, and there because they pray, as they do, to the Blessed Virgin Mary? We ought to be too thankful that the *prayers themselves* sympathize with us, that providentially no false doctrine is inserted *there.*

Of course, you spread the papers you send me before Him, and pray over them.

## LETTER CVI.

### Oversights not to be brooded over.

My very dear Child in our Lord,

. . . . . For the rest, I do not say dismiss the oversight altogether from your mind, but I most earnestly say, "Do not worry yourself about it." Let it stand as one of the faults, by God's mercy, forgiven, and not to be dwelt upon in detail, but only recollected in its general substance as a reason for clinging more and more to the gracious Saviour, who thus shews us to ourselves, and what we might (or rather would surely) be without Him. The rest when we meet. In the meantime, do not grudge yourself His holy comfort.

Ever y$^r$ very loving,
J. K.

## LETTER CVII.

### Sadness in Devotion not always Wrong.

My very dear Child,

I really cannot remember exactly what special place it was in George Herbert which I happened to quote to you. I think the point was to shew, it is not, in every sense, wrong to be sad in our devotions; and yet that seems to me so very obvious, were it only from the Psalms, and still more from the Gospels, that I cannot imagine how any one could have taught the contrary. Perhaps I might refer you to that called "Affliction," which begins "my heart did heave;" which seems to suggest as a kind of test of the sadness, that you should give it a religious turn, make it an exercise in taking up the Cross. Then there is "Bitter and Sweet," and on the other hand, "The Method," "The Glance," "The Size;" any of which, in its turn, may chance to help you.

My dear wife, D. G., has not had her spasm again, though she suffers much from her back: but now we are to have all our rooms on a ground-floor. And, as yet, the climate is tolerable. It was my fault your not getting a proper farewell of her: I let you go, and when she asked for you, you were got too far off. So lay the blame on your loving old friend,

J. K.

As to the sparks of vanity and fretfulness, and other feelings of self, which you complain of, tread them out, my Child, as fast as they arise, by daily confession, as in the Lord's Prayer especially, when they relate to ———.

o

# LETTER CVIII.

### To a Gentleman who had Consulted him about a Change of Profession, and taking Holy Orders.

CONCERNING your scheme, one can feel nothing but joy and thankfulness that such a thought should have come into your heart. It startled me, I own, at first; but on coming to ask myself why, I really believe that this was only from its being so new and unusual a thing, though, in a certain sense, it may seem very old: for who knows but it may have been put into your mind for the same kind of purpose, which made so many of our forefathers, of all ages and stations, enter the religious life. I do not, of course, compare the two, but may it not be in our day the same *kind* of thing in some measure? This I say to myself to meet the scruple you hint at, and which a great many would feel, about being less useful so, than as a layman trying his best. It seems to me that this would be more to the purpose, if you cut short your active professional life for the sake of doing this; but it would not be so; it would be something substituted for miscellaneous, and not strictly professional work, and in that respect would perhaps involve a good deal of self-denial; of course, you will consider well beforehand, whether, applying yourself, as you would wish to do, to your new profession, you will have leisure for the many calls for time and thought, which are sure to be made on you, in your retirement. You will not like to put them by; and I can fancy them going on, on such a large scale, as to interfere seriously with your pastoral work.

I only mention this for consideration; there may be nothing in it, your habits being so active.

The testimony, both as regards religion generally, and faith in our own Church particularly, would, as it seems to me, be the stronger in such a change, than in a person's continuing a dutiful layman.

On the whole (I have been just reading over your letter again), I am much inclined to say, go on and prosper, and may a great blessing attend you.


# LETTER CIX.

## ON SELF-DENIAL.

MY DEAR CHILD,

I send you a few hints; you will consider whether they are likely to do you good: and mention to me freely anything that occurs to you.

In the matter of self-denial, I may mention that perhaps your studies of various kinds may give you room for some exercises of the kind; you may set yourself a strict rule to break off what you are about, though it be never so interesting, as the solution of a question in Algebra, or something very critical in a novel—when the time comes for religious exercise. I think it was John Wesley who set himself and others such strict rules against the "lust of finishing." A peaceful Lent to you, dear Child, and a happy Easter.

Your loving Father in Christ,

J. K.

## LENT.

1. Settle within yourself some particular sin to be fought against, or grace to be practised, during this Lent, especially : e.g. suppose the sin Pride, and the grace Humility.

2. Begin the day on waking with an act of prayer for one and against the other: e.g. the three first verses of Psalm cxxxi.

3. Meditate (with the help of writing if you find it better) for at least a quarter of an hour daily, at such time as you may find best (I should say as near morning prayer as may be convenient) on some text, or anecdote, or parabolical circumstance read of or observed, bearing on the special subject.

4. Add to your devotions at one or more of the hours (say sext or nones), some such form as this :

Lord, have mercy, &c.

Our Father, &c.

Text.  Whosoever exalteth himself, &c.

Thanks be to God.

Lord, let me not be high minded.

*Let me have no proud looks.*

Let me refrain my soul and keep it low.

*Like as a child that is weaned from his mother.*

Lord, hear my prayer.

*And let my cry come unto Thee.*

O God be merciful to me a sinner, and look on me with those eyes of mercy wherewith Thou didst behold the Publican; that by true humility in heart, word, and deed, I may obtain grace to be justified before Thee, and exalted among Thy faithful ones; through Jesus Christ our Lord. *Amen.*

# LETTER CX.

### AGAINST DESPONDENCY IN RESPECT TO ONE'S PRAYERS.

..... IT is very distressing, and I feel greatly for you; but you must not give way to anything like despondency. Your tendency, as you well know, is to do so, in your prayers, as well as in other things, the imagination haunts you of its being all "no good." I should like you to try this time, whether you can meet the trial by earnest "practice of the presence of God:" e.g. whenever and wherever you receive this, try to fix your mind on this certain truth, that our Lord is watching to see how you read it, and just ask Him, as heartily as you can, to be with you and help you when the time comes for evening prayer. When that time comes, open your Bible on your knees, and look earnestly on some such verse as, "I am He that trieth the reins and the hearts;" or, "Do not I fill heaven and earth?" &c.; then shut your eyes, and try to think of Him as really present, asking His help to do so : then go on and say, "O, Good Saviour, grant me this once to say my prayers to Thee dutifully" (or some such words); then go on with your usual exercise, remembering to ask particularly for grace to pray the next morning ; and when that morning comes, repeat the same process, varying (if you like) words and text, &c. : and so on for a week, and send me word how it answers. For a penance, I scarcely know what to recommend ; the only thing which occurs to me is, whether it might be well (if not too sharp) to confess it to —— or ——, and make a rule to do so if it recurred : but this should not be done in a hurry. I only *mention*, I do not *recommend* it. But it must be good to ask our Lord to teach you Himself how to do penance. Go to Him unreservedly, trust Him, He will surely help you. In great haste,

Your very loving Father in Xt.,

J. K.

# LETTER CXI.

## ON JOINING AN ASSOCIATION FOR UNITED PRAYER.

MY DEAR CHILD,

. . . . . I am not myself one of the Association you speak of, nor do I know very much about it. My unpunctual forgetful habits have always made me shrink from engagements of that kind, as knowing too well what small chance there was of my tolerably fulfilling them. In spirit, one hopes that one does so, after a sort, by trying to mean what one says in one's daily prayers in church or at home. I am rather inclined to think that in your case the engagement might have the general good effect you speak of, by enabling you to attend better to your other prayers. But take care that what you pledge yourself to shall take up very little time; and perhaps it will help you to connect the prayer, from time to time, with the thought of some particular person who may seem to need such charitable help. It may be worth considering, too, about engaging oneself, in the first instance, for a time only. As to that old difficulty, I will just mention that one troubled in that way seemed very much to welcome the notion of dividing and sub-dividing her devotions —a very little, but very often. Did you ever try anything of the kind? Would you mind writing me a line or two, when you are able, to report on the effect of these or other suggestions? or ideas which may occur to you?

This air was recommended to us as being very temperate and soothing, though very moist. . . . . It is a beautiful bit of coast, pleasant drives when weather allows, sober and comfortable church services *daily,* and several kind friends, who know how to be cordial but not intrusive. So on the whole we are very comfortable: only *it is not Hursley.* . . .

## LETTER CXII.

### ON DISINCLINATION TO PRAYER.

I HAVE loitered so, my dear Child, that I am almost afraid this cannot reach you before Christmas Day, and, in any case, it will be too tardy. But I will say what I can now, and if more occurs, you shall have it, D.V. To begin with what is of most consequence, I think you should not be broken-hearted when that dislike of your prayers comes on. It should put you, *first,* on being very thankful for the quiet time that has gone before, in the quantity of which you seem to be more favoured than very many; *secondly,* on considering carefully whether anything in your behaviour, inward or outward, may have occurred, which may, in part at least, cause it, tempting the devil, as it were, to tempt you. (For although Scripture does not say that he or any created being can read our hearts, I suppose that he is keen to watch every glance, tone, and movement, and to take advantage of the feeling or temper which it may betoken.) Thirdly, both the thanksgiving and the prayer to be helped in the examination, should be direct acts of devotion. It might be well to draw up forms of words, never mind how simple, against the next trial, or when you begin to be tried, and force yourself to say them, and, as much as you can, to feel that you mean them; for you know you do so in the bottom of your heart. You have no wish to leave off prayer, for good and all. Then, if God gives you the sense of thankfulness, or helps you to a sight of what has interrupted you, the spell is so far broken, and most likely you will be able to go on and pray as usual. If not, still a sign will have been made, which will be sure to bring an answer sooner or later, and it will be your duty to go on with your *forms* of prayer—forcing yourself, in spite of any disgust you seem to feel, and helping yourself at frequent intervals with such exclamations as a drowning man might use, " God, forgive me ;" " Father, forgive, for I know not what I am doing ;" "Lord, save me, I perish," &c. And pray beforehand, and at the time, against the power and presence of the Evil One ; for one cannot but apprehend that he has a great deal to do with such cases. It might be well, perhaps, at the first consciousness of such a trouble, very solemnly to place yourself in our Lord's presence, make the sign of the Cross, and use some grave kind of exorcism, such as, " In the Name of, &c., depart from me, thou bad Spirit; and do Thou, O Lord, have mercy upon me." In your Christmas devotions you will, I am sure, present this great and sore trouble very earnestly before your Saviour; and you need not fear to come near Him for pardon and help—did He not come on purpose to break such bands? I hope (D.V.) to think earnestly of you? I shall be anxious to hear soon how it is with you, and if anything more comes into my head that seems worth writing, I will be sure, please God, to write. . . . . The best of Christmas blessings be with you, dear Child.

Ever yours,

J. K.

### FOR ONE TEMPTED TO OMIT PRAYER.

Bring my soul out of prison that I may give thanks unto Thy Name.

Psalm cxliii. (Hear my prayer, O Lord, and consider.)

Bring my soul, &c.

Lord, have mercy.

Christ, have mercy.

Lord, have mercy.

Our Father, &c.

For a small moment have I forsaken thee, but with great mercies will I gather thee.

LESSON. Micah vii. 7—9.

Therefore I will look unto the Lord; I will wait for the God of my salvation: my God will hear me.

Rejoice not against me, O mine enemy: when I fall, I shall arise; when I sit in darkness, the Lord shall be a light unto me.

I will bear the indignation of the Lord, because I have sinned against Him, until He plead my cause, and execute judgment for me: He will bring me forth to the light, and I shall behold His righteousness.

For a small moment.

### Collects.

O Lord, we beseech Thee mercifully to hear us, and grant that we, to whom Thou hast given an hearty desire to pray, may by Thy mighty aid be freed from the interruptions of the evil one, and defended in all dangers and adversities, through Jesus Christ our Lord. *Amen.*

℣. I said, Lord, be merciful unto me:

℟. Heal my soul, for I have sinned against Thee.

Almighty and most gracious God, Who for Thy people in their drought didst bring living water out of the rock, cause we beseech Thee our hard and dry hearts to give forth penitential tears, that we may be able to mourn for our sins, and made meet by Thy mercy to obtain forgiveness, through Jesus Christ our Lord. *Amen.*

# LETTER CXIII.

## TO ONE ON THE EVE OF HIS ORDINATION.

MY DEAR ——,

When I think on what a point in your life you are come to, and what a nothing I have done for you, I, who was so bound, on so many accounts, to do my very best, I feel as if I ought to tremble ; and at last, though now at the eleventh hour, I must write you one little line, with such a blessing as I can send, if it be but to shew you that you are not quite forgotten.

My dear ——, take the word of one who knows, by sad experience, that there is no comfort for an ordained person, but in really striving, night and day, to keep his Ordination vows, and especially that one, in which we bind ourselves to frame and fashion our lives according to the doctrine of Christ : i.e. really and truly to lead holy lives — to please Him in thought, word, and deed.   I mention this so particularly, because, obvious as it is, I know that in the excitement of entering on a new state of life, and in laying one's self out, as a kind and honourable mind naturally will, in waiting on others, there is too much danger of a person's neglecting himself, though his general intentions be good.   Take my word for it, your first and chief business will be to keep yourself in order : I mean, especially, your senses and thoughts ; if they be duly guarded, all the rest will be blessed ; if they be indulged and let to run wild, you may do much good, and seem exemplary, yet all will be poisoned and blighted within, and if you are saved, it will be so as by fire.

God grant that this, which is a real and sad truth, may take fast hold of your heart, now in the beginning of your ministry, that you may be a true penitent before you put your hand to the Ark.

Many will befriend and pray for you, were it only for your dear Father's sake ; do not you forget to befriend and pray for yourself. I send you this little book, who wrote it I do not well know, but some such help seems especially needful for those who are to guide others.

## LETTER CXIV.

### A Word on the Study of the Fathers.

I MUST say one word as to your remark that it is startling to find our friends go off, as they come to know more of the Fathers. It *would be* startling, if it were not accompanied, as it avowedly is, both in N. and W., and I suppose in all the rest, with a growing disdain of the authority of the Fathers, and a substitution of the later Church for them.

P., who, I imagine, knows as much of the Fathers as any one, finds his old faith strengthened by them, because he does not shift his ground, substituting, as they do, Development for Tradition.

## LETTER CXV.

### SACRAMENTAL CONFESSION NOT TO BE OF SINGLE SINS ONLY.

ABOUT Confession: do you not think there is a good deal in what is commonly alleged, that the Rubric directs Confession, not of the particular matter which troubles him only, but of " his sins?" and also in the reason assigned, that one part of the character is so linked on with another, that a Director cannot well enjoin penance, or give advice, or indeed judge about giving Absolution, without such a general view of the case as that saying imports. The degree of detail is left to his judgment, I conceive.

My own feeling would be, that if a person does not feel up to stating his whole case, I should bid him be content with the general Absolutions, applying them to his own case; advising him, of course, as well as I could from the partial view he gave me.

I should not call this, refusing Absolution.

I have not read what Mr. —— writes, but if he thinks he has a right to pronounce *that* Absolution upon Confession not of the man's *" sins,"* but of that

one only, or more, which he selects for Confession,
I consider it a very dangerous mistake of the Church's
meaning.

## LETTER CXVI.

### On the Presence of Non-Communicants at the Holy Eucharist.

. . . . I CANNOT deny that I have a strong feeling
against the foreign custom of encouraging *all sorts
of persons* to "assist" at the Holy Eucharist, without communicating. It seems to me open to two
grave objections: it cannot be without danger of
profaneness and irreverence to very many, and of
consequent dishonour to the Holy Sacrament: and
it has brought in and encouraged, or both, (at least
so I greatly suspect), a notion of a quasi-sacramental
virtue in such attendance, which I take to be great
part of the error stigmatized in our 31st Article.
Even in such a good book as the *Imitatio Christi*,
and still more in the *Paradisus Animæ*, one finds
participating "in Missâ *vel* Communione," spoken of
as if one brought a spiritual benefit of the same
order as the other. This I believe to be utterly un-
authorized by Scripture and Antiquity; and I can
imagine it of very dangerous consequence. But
whatever one thought of this, the former objection
would still stand, and it would not do to answer that
the early Church allowed, or even encouraged, the

practice, because, even if that were granted, (I very much doubt it, to say the least), the existence of discipline at that time entirely alters the case. I used to argue in this way with poor R. W., but I could never get him to mind me.

Yet of course I cannot deny that there may be any number of cases in which attendance without communicating may be morally and spiritually (I could not say, sacramentally) beneficial: and in default of discipline, I should advise any person who thought that such was his own case, to consult with his Spiritual Adviser, and act accordingly: the clergyman of the particular church not objecting.

I am very sorry for what you say of ——'s case; but I could expect no other, from his shewing himself so palpably one-sided as he had done before.

The wish for an infallible guide to relieve one of responsibility, is plainly very natural, but as plainly not intended to be granted in this world.

God be with you, dear Mr. ——.

Believe me, ever affec^tly yours,

J. KEBLE.

# LETTER[h] CXVII.

### ON THE REAL PRESENCE IN THE HOLY EUCHARIST.

You do not, I trust, consider me or my friends who are in the same case to be maintaining our interpretation as the only admissible one in the Church of England. We are forced in reason and conscience to ask leave to hold it ourselves, as seeming to us more probable than any other: but we are not enforcing it as a condition of Communion—far otherwise. We have been put on the defensive, and there, unless we could see that we have erred, we must try to make our stand. I cannot believe that you would think it a duty to expel us, though it is plain that a great many do.

Now I will try and say what my belief is: and you, my dear friend, of your charity will bear with me if what I say grates upon your inward ear.

1. I believe that there is One, and only One True Body of the Lord Jesus, in the sense in which any man's natural body is called his own: That Body, namely, which He took of the Blessed Virgin Mary when He came into the world.

2. That neither this Body, nor the Reasonable Soul which He took to Himself at the same time, nor His Manhood, consisting of both together, have,

---

[h] The letter, from which this is an extract, is of considerable length, but the part that follows what is here given, is of a theological and controversial character, unsuited to this Collection.

or ever had, any distinct Personality, but have subsisted, and ever will subsist, as taken into the Person of the Word, the Eternal Son of God.

3. That as the Divine Word, or Person of Christ, is everywhere and always Present and Adorable; so ever since the Incarnation, the Presence of the Body of Christ, or the Presence of the Soul of Christ, or of Both united, whenever and wherever and however He vouchsafes to notify it, is to be taken as a warrant and a call for especial Adoration on the part of all His reasonable creatures, to whom the knowledge of His Two Natures has been vouchsafed,—Adoration to Him as to God Most High, and to His Holy Manhood, not separately, but as subsisting in His Divine Person.  I believe, therefore,

4. That His sacrificed Body, hanging on the Cross and laid in the grave, was adorable.

5. I understand the words, "This is My Body, which is $\left\{ \begin{array}{c} \text{given} \\ \text{broken} \end{array} \right\}$ for you," *literally taken*, as declaring His Eucharistical Body, or That which He gives us as the inward part of the Sacrament, to be the same Body which was sacrificed.

6. And I believe that those words ought to be literally taken : Therefore,

7. I believe His Eucharistical Body, or That which He gives us as the inward part of the Sacrament, to be adorable.

It seems to me that the only questionable link

in this chain, for one who believes the Nicene and Athanasian Creeds, is the last but one; "Those words should be taken literally." Granting all the rest, it might still be questioned, May not the words mean only, "This is a figure of My Body?" or, "This is (not My Body, but) something which in energy and effect will be *as it were* My Body?" The former of these, I suppose, to be the Zuinglian view, the latter the Calvinistic. Besides these two, I see no way of taking the words short of the literal one. But neither of these two will bear the weight of the 6th Chapter of St. John, or of the sayings of the ancient Church, especially in the Liturgies. Therefore I fall back on the literal sense, which makes it necessary for me to allow Adoration, or deny the "taking of the Manhood into God."

The difference between the Eucharistical Presence, and the Presence in holy places and assemblies, I should have thought, was something like this; that in the latter, our Lord's Body (of course I speak not of His Mystical Body) is present only in such manner as Hooker defines, E. P., v. 55, 7[1]; in the former, as St. Ambrose writes, "Christ is there *because* the Body of Christ is there."

---

[1] "The *Person of Christ is whole*, perfect God and perfect Man, wheresoever, although the parts of His Manhood being finite, and His Deity infinite, we cannot say that the *whole of Christ* is simply everywhere, as we may say that His Deity is, and that His person is, by force of Deity."—*Hooker, Eccl. Pol.*, v. chap. 55, 7.

## LETTER CXVIII.

### ON RESERVATION FOR COMMUNION OF THE SICK.

As to your rubrical case, I must frankly own that I think —— has the best of the argument. It is a matter on which many times I have wished, and still wish, the Rubric altered, but I cannot deny that (right or wrong) it is as express as possible. . . . . Of· course it is a privation not to receive the Holy Sacrament with the rest of His people, on His own great days: but it would be balanced in my mind by the feeling, that in the other course I was disobeying the Church : and it is something that, by deferring the private communion to some other day in the Octave, you double, as it were, your own Easter Communion.

Perhaps this may help to reconcile —— to the sacrifice she will have to make, should you, on reflection, come to view the matter in this way.

To me it is a great satisfaction that we have been from time to time getting a little nearer to the old reverential ways in this, as in many other points; as any one may see, who will compare with one another the Rubric concerning the Remains in Edward's and Elizabeth's time with that in the present Prayer-book.

## LETTER CXIX.

### ON CELIBACY AS A COUNSEL OF PERFECTION.

YOUR letters imply two things: first, that Scripture gives no encouragement to persons to devote themselves to a single life, as more angelical, and enabling them to wait on their Lord with less distraction. And again, that at any rate this is not a case for such preference. On the first of these points I feel *quite sure* that you are under a mistake. Our Lord's words (which your letters do not notice) are so very express: and in all reason St. Paul's must be interpreted by them: and this has been the interpretation, not of one or two writers only, nor of one or two generations only, but of the whole Church from the beginning. I will only just mention two writers, to whom, perhaps, we owe as much deference as any—Hooker and Herbert. Hooker says, "Single life is a thing more Angelical and Divine:" and Herbert says, "Inasmuch as Virginity is a higher state than Matrimony, and the Ministry requires the best and holiest things, the Country Parson is rather unmarried than married." Both these were married men, and both far enough from Popery. . . .

# LETTER CXX.

## ON VOWS OF CELIBACY.

MY DEAR MR. ——,

I am sorry to write so tardily, and more sorry to be of no real use to you, as I am conscious must be the case.

The poor little scrap which I send with this, contains a few references ᵏ, such as I have been able to make out, being myself rather behindhand in engagements of my own at present. I should suppose—

1. That there were professed Virgins—whether under perpetual vows or not, does not seem clear—from the beginning, as a kind of *class*, not *order*, in the Church.

2. That vows of Virginity were allowed and were binding.

3. Perhaps there were Sisterhoods; much more probably than not.

On the whole, celibacy was greatly encouraged, but great caution required in professing it. Vows once made, whether in public or in private, were

---

ᵏ The references here alluded to, are such as Mr. Keble had leisure just then to set down for the consideration of his correspondent, whom he evidently considered to be better acquainted with the subject than he was himself. They are to various passages in the early Fathers, and to Canons of ancient Councils. They are not given here, as, to be of any use, they must be extracted at length, and would give quite a different character to the letter, from that of the rest of the collection.—ED.

binding, and the breach of them a sin. Compare St. Matt. xix. 12, and by way of limitation, the principle in Numbers xxx. I fancy a great deal might be gathered out of St. Augustine and the Post-Nicene writers, to shew the secondary uses of the ascetic life, for works of Charity, &c.; but these hints, such as they are, seem all to relate to its primary end, as a counsel of perfection; which doctrine all those ages appear to have accepted most unreservedly.

Forgive this meagre note, and believe me always, dear Mr. ——,

Truly and affectionately yours,<br>J. KEBLE.

What a case this is of coals to Newcastle!

## LETTER CXXI.

### ON THE RELIGIOUS REVIVALS IN IRELAND.

MY DEAR ——,

Perhaps the simplest way of trying to give one's thoughts on this very serious matter will be to take ——'s *favourable* statement as the correct account, and mention what occurs to one on reading it, and thinking it over, in connexion with the *sure* Word of God.

1. "God at this time is shedding His Holy Spirit in a marvellous way on His people," &c. But is

He not *always* doing so, since Pentecost, according to our Lord's promises on the Eve of His Death, and according to the whole tenor of the Gospel? Are not all Christians in a supernatural state, as Israel was in the wilderness, whether they will believe and act on it or no? If anything more is meant than the sanctification assured to all members of Christ who apply for it in earnest, then surely it is a new dispensation, something over and above the Gospel. And then, what would St. Paul say to it? See Gal. i. 8.

It is well that the Belfast miracles are disclaimed: but certainly if there is a new Pentecost, or something more, one might expect from God's former doings that there would be new miracles to announce it, and so far the Belfast people are the more consistent.

2. "He who is acted on receives a clear knowledge that his sins are pardoned, that He is in God's near favour, and is among those who are saved," &c. That is, in the place of miracles we have personal assurance: each one's own personal assurance that he is in God's near favour is a proof to himself, and the great number of persons having that feeling, is, or ought to be, a proof to the world.

Now I take it for granted that the good people who have this sort of conviction would be far from either thinking, or teaching, that it is to supersede the plain letter of the Word of God, in such places as, "If thou wilt enter into life *keep* the commandments;" "Blessed are they that *do* His commandments:" "This is the love of God, that we *keep* His commandments." "By their *fruits* ye shall know them," and "the fruit of the Spirit is," &c. &c.

What then will they say to any person, who, trying himself by these standards, and not having the least doubt of God's love to him, or that Christ died for him, and that he has received the Holy Spirit, is yet in fear and trembling (though *not* in despair, God forbid), because of his much ingratitude and many sins, and would really be afraid to pray for, and trust, any such personal undoubting assurance, lest it should lessen his contrition, or even encourage him to take liberties. Would they say that such an one was outside the covenant of grace, &c.? Yet who would an unprejudiced reader say reminded him most of her whom we know to have been most highly favoured?—or of him who counted not himself to have obtained, but kept saying to himself, "What if I should myself be a castaway?" In short, the whole of this doctrine of the necessity of assurance is to me not left doubtful, but contradicted, by such places as Philippians ii. 12, 13; indeed, by the whole Gospel, our Lord's own teaching in particular: and I pray God to keep us all from it.

3. As to the effects[1]—God forbid one should dis-

---

[1] Extract from the letter on which Mr. Keble was commenting. "Young men in the full vigour of life, in enjoyment of robust health

parage any of His Works in any way, and we know
that all truth and goodness is His Work: but is it
not begging the question, to infer that these doctrines
are from Him? because they who embrace them
are better than they were? Suppose I shew you
a Roman Catholic who has become such from being
a Jew, and at the same [time ?] was really converted
from the love of the world to the love of God, would
you say at once, this proves that the worship of the
Virgin, &c., comes from God? No: you would say,
and that truly, that no one could ever tell but that
the improvement was owing to the grace of God
coming and blessing the Faith by which this person
received, not that particular doctrine, but the great
Truths of the Creed common to all Christianity.
This seems to me to apply to the present case.
Persons "not eminent for concern about the truths
of religion" suddenly devote themselves to good
things, feeling in themselves, in a way unknown to

and all abundance, fond of all manly exercises, and not remarkable
for any intellectual attainments or concern about the truths of religion,
suddenly devote themselves to the study of God's Word, and to indoc-
trinating others with their own convictions. They give up manly
amusements of which they were fond, and devote all their leisure to
religious proselytism.    They read their Bibles with much diligence,
and sit up late at night, conferring with one another, enlarging on
their own Spiritual condition, and praying. This is the great subject
of their conversation and correspondence. They organize religious
meetings, they press home on the careless, or cold and formal, the
necessity of a renewal and revival   Meanwhile they are attentive to
their own duties and conduct."

them before, how true and great these things are:
but might not people, and do they not often, take
the same good turn, without its being recommended
by this doctrine of "personal assurance?" The reformation may be due to truths in which all Christians agree, not to this notion, at best newly and
partially revealed.

Moreover, I cannot say that the list of good fruits
here given is to me quite satisfactory. New con-
verts cannot, I think, without some spiritual im-
propriety and danger, "give all their leisure to religious proselytism."

In the only case of sudden conversion related with
any detail in the New Testament, though it was
evidently a rare and miraculous work, there was
deep penance, much solitude, submission (where God
did not directly inspire) to the advice of those who
were disciples before. As to the conversions at large
(see Acts ii., and elsewhere), plainly the persons were
putting themselves altogether under the direction
of the Apostles, and their doing so was a necessary token that they were of God, (St. Matt. x. 40 ;
1 St. John iv. 6). I read of people keeping Church
vigils (Acts xx. 7—11), but I do not read of
"young men suddenly converted" sitting up late
at night, conferring with one another, enlarging on
their own spiritual condition ; nor of their organiz-
ing religious meetings, &c., where there were already
regular elders ordained by Timothy and Titus.

Much less do I read of their disparaging watchfulness, or imagining that they do right as of course.

These are my thoughts upon what —— calls the "favourable" side of his statement. As to the other side, I am sorry to say that I cannot find anything to abate in what he says of the certain tendencies of such an opinion in respect of doctrine and Church practices, and of the possibility of Satan transforming himself into an Angel of light in this case as in so many others [m]. The goodness and piety of the persons concerned in such a thing, at any special time, or in any special instance, is no proof

---

[m] The sum of their Theology is God's work in themselves. For further doctrines or substantial faith, there is, I suppose, none. They need neither learning nor study. What they hold is God's truth by personal inspiration, through study of the Bible. "They have an unction from the Holy One, and know all things." I suppose they would accept the personal application of this text, not only as for the saving of their own souls, but as making them guides and teachers of God's people to bring them to a knowledge of His truth. The Church, with its organization and ministry, creeds, ordinances and sacraments, would come before them very much as formal. The hidden life-giving grace, the renewing of the soul, would be sought elsewhere, by what would seem to them more direct communion with God. Until their hearts have been visited with this spiritual revival, they regard themselves and others as outside the covenant of Grace.

Can it be a device of the Evil One? He tries all ways of deceit: he can transform himself into an Angel of light. May not a trial of the latter days be a delusive representation of God's truth, so as to draw people away from the faith once for all delivered to the saints, and by sowing divisions and substituting error to check the progress of Christ's Kingdom, corrupt His truth, and carry away people after a phantom? So that in truth he may be gradually substituting another Gospel for that which Christ and His Apostles taught.

that the proper "fruit," i.e. the *tendency* of the thing, is good.

Simple and loving Faith may draw the sting of the mischief from a few earnest and *humble* souls, but the question is,—What will be the effect on the average sort of the sons and daughters of Adam? I say this especially with reference to one topic which —— has touched on—the regarding one's self or others as outside the Covenant of Grace, and of course destitute of its privileges, before this conscious revival has taken place. People who have been taught this—how will they look upon their old sins? You and I know too well by the sort of sayings we hear by the side of many death-beds :—"Oh, Sir, he's quite happy:" and yet the man's life may have been very irreligious, and the signs of repentance only just such as not entirely to exclude hope. They could not take it so, if they had not a kind of instinct which makes them presume on human assurance, as if it were indeed Christ's token : which is just what this doctrine encourages them to do. From whom can such instinct come? The Spirit of loving, patient obedience may and will save sincere Christians, leading good lives, independently of this doctrine, from such use of it; yet logically it is the legitimate use, and the Adversary knows it but too well.

To put the whole in two lines ;—Why is our people's standard of goodness so low, but because they undervalue their Baptismal Privileges? and this doctrine indorses that sentiment and makes it a duty. It warrants in all cases what I once heard a Dissenter say in one case;—when he was told of his boy telling lies, he said very calmly, "You know, Sir, all have not the same grace." If that boy grew up and ever got "converted," in this sense, I should fear he thought little of the lies he had told before; he would hardly say the fifty-first Psalm in the sense in which the Church by the Holy Spirit has always taught her penitents to say it. He could hardly go on in the spirit of that verse,—"I acknowledge my faults, and my sin is ever before me:" he could hardly pray continually with the Church, "Create and make in me a new and *contrite* heart." And as for such as are unconverted, and believe themselves so, they are sure almost to draw the conclusion, that their time being not yet come to serve God, their sins do not so much signify.

But after all, the great argument is the want of Scripture authority for this need of special assurance: without *that*, be its effects bad or good, it cannot be other than a new Gospel. And then we know what to think of it.

I am ever yours very aff<sup>ly</sup>,<br>
J. KEBLE.

1861.

# LETTER CXXII.

## ON THE BURIAL OFFICE.

*Written at the request of the late Bishop of Exeter,*
*who says in a letter,*

"It was written at my request, after an earnest conversation with him, when the matter was to be brought before the House of Lords. I think you will value it, as I do, most highly."

I SUPPOSE that it would be a true account of the Office for the Burial of the Dead in our Prayer-book, to say that it is intended to set forth the mind of the Church, which is the mind of Christ, in regard of those who have died, being Members of His Mystical Body. To call it a Form for the Burial of the Body hardly expresses its full meaning. It is a Form surely of commending the whole person, body and soul, to Almighty God; of bidding the departed farewell, and leaving him in his Saviour's holy keeping. Accordingly, in King Edward's first Prayer-book, the Priest, casting earth upon the corpse, was to say, "I commend thy soul to God the Father Almighty, and thy body to the ground; earth to earth," &c. And in the Collect afterwards, "We commend into Thy Hands of Mercy, most merciful Father, the soul of this our brother departed, *N.* And his body we commit

to the earth; beseeching Thine infinite goodness
... that ... both this our brother and we may be
found acceptable in Thy sight." And, "We give
Thee hearty thanks for this Thy servant, whom Thou
hast delivered from the miseries of this wretched
world, from the body of death, and all temptation ;
and, as we trust, hast brought his soul, which he
committed into Thy holy Hands, into sure consolation and rest.   Grant, we beseech Thee, that at the
day of judgment his soul, and all the souls of Thine
elect, departed out of this life, may with us, and we
with them, fully receive Thy Promises, and be made
perfect altogether."

These expressions have been some of them modified : but *not, assuredly, with any intention of throw-
ing doubt on the Church's view of our present communion with our brethren departed.*   On the contrary, it stands to reason, that if the Church for the
time thought it expedient to withdraw her pre-
scribed forms of intercession for them, she would
have us the more earnest and affectionate in retain-
ing all unobjectionable memorials of them.   At any
rate, in neither of the Offices is any more question
made of their being still within the Communion of
Saints, than there is of the living congregation being
all rightly called "Brethren," and "good Christian
people ;" all prayed for as such, all invited to the
Holy Altar-Table ;—no more question than St. Paul
made in his denominating the Roman Christians,

collectively, " beloved of God, called to be Saints,"
or the Corinthians and others, " Saints," and " sanctified in Christ Jesus," and " faithful Brethren." So
much as this, is ingrained, as it were, in the very
texture of the whole service. You do not get rid
of it by altering any single expressions, such as those
which are sometimes objected to. If the objections
be allowed, we have but two alternatives : either
there must be no service at all, or it must be toned
down to the simplest acknowledgment, such as a
Deist might perhaps make, of God's over-ruling Providence. *It could not be Scriptural,* for *Holy Scrip-*
*ture* everywhere (as we know on the highest authority) implies the continued personal existence of
the Dead, and *some communion between them and*
*the living.*

Suppose the Service analysed in detail, with a
view to this account of its general drift. Why, first
of all, is the body brought to consecrated ground—
ground set apart as especially belonging to Christ
—and there met by one of Christ's representatives ?
Why, but because it is to be committed to Christ's
keeping, and He accepts the charge of it ? He, the
same Christ, that had once vouchsafed to take it
up in His arms and bless it ; whose gifts and calling
are declared to be without repentance.

Next, the Church, assuming (as all along in the
person's lifetime) that *the Baptismal blessing has not*
*been finally forfeited,* repeats after her Lord the

Q

words of promise depending on that assumption.
There is the promise of continued life as well to
the departed as to the surviving believer : " He that
believeth in Me, though he were dead, yet shall he
live ; and whosoever liveth and believeth in Me shall
never die." There is also the promise of the Resurrection of the Body, to behold with the very same
eyes the returning Saviour : " He shall stand at the
latter day upon the earth ; and though after my
skin worms destroy this body, yet in my flesh shall
I see God : whom I shall see for myself, and mine
eyes shall behold and not another." The common
anticipation of that sight is a far greater thing to
bind the survivors to the departed, than death and
burial and decay to separate them.

Then, following her loving Saviour in such sympathy as He shewed by His Tears over the grave
of Lazarus, and by His Compassion on the Widow
of Nain, the Church does, in a manner, condole with
her departed child, and with the rest who are soon
to depart, on their sad helplessness and desolation
in the moment of Death, *naturally* considered ; "We
brought nothing," &c. But she makes haste again,
as at Nain and at Bethany, to console them : " The
Lord gave," &c. As if she should say, "This is the
message which I have of Him to declare unto you,
'Trust thy departed ones with Me : living and dying
they are Mine : I do but summon them from one
room in My house to another.'"

The appointed Psalms of course take up and continue the melody, mingling our Lord's lesson to
the living with His merciful sympathies towards the
Dead; putting into our mouths the strains of resignation and hope, which yesterday were the solace
of those who are gone; so as to make us feel that
we are but going on with the service which they
left unfinished.  And in the Lesson, all, dead and
living alike, are called to hear by Faith the voice
of the Archangel and the trump of God.  It ·is
printed on the soul as with lightning, that *we without them, and they without us, cannot by any means
be made perfect;* that our Communion, sealed by
Death, is inseparable for ever.

Strengthened by such a revelation, the Christian
mourner comes to the most trying moment of all;
and a word of sympathy is provided for him again
from the Book of Job: that Book of the Old Testament, which peculiarly exhibits the compassion of
the Almighty towards the most humiliating and repul-
sive forms of human misery: "Man that is born," &c.
And the accompanying prayer or hymn, true to the
tone of all Christian Antiquity, is so worded as almost
to turn itself into a prayer for the Departed, as well
as for the survivors.  At least, if such a thought
should.occur to any one using the Prayer, it has been
ruled, I believe, on high authority, that he need not
suppress it, as undutiful to the English Church.  And
probably he would but be praying as St. Paul might

by the grave of Onesiphorus. Now in whatever mode or degree such intercession is allowed or allowable in the English Church, so far, plainly, the Burial Office will be a Form of Communion with the Dead, not simply of warning, consolation, and prayer for the living.

In the solemn Proclamation, for instance, which accompanies the actual interment, the "sure and certain Hope," of course refers to the Article of the Creed. But is it in human nature to assist in that service without a secret wish (and a wish breathed to God is a prayer), that so it may prove when *this* grave comes to be opened?

Observe, too, the text, part of which follows as an anthem; especially if it be rendered more exactly according to the original: "Blessed are the dead which die in the Lord *from that moment*:" i.e. I suppose their blessedness begins *immediately;* "yea, saith the Spirit, that they may rest" (or perhaps, "in a place where they shall rest") "from their labours; but their works are following with them," (="attending on them"?). What a deep interest are we here invited to take in their present condition! What a distinct idea (in one respect) of the nature of their happiness is presented! Their *labours* are no more —it is perfect tranquillity: but their works—the fruits of their labours—follow on with them; the effects of their devout practice and holy obedience abide in their hearts and in their heavenly or Paradisaïcal lives. This saying, thoughtfully received, may by God's mercy do much towards lessening the weary interval between the bereaved and the Departed.

The prayers which follow will give more entire relief, now that we have warrant of God's Word for believing, that as we sympathize in our measure with our brother's "joy and felicity," and give thanks for his deliverance out of "this sinful world," so he, who, in character, is still what he was, and what God's co-operating grace had made him, does in far higher perfection still sympathize with us in our prayers,—still cries out with the Church on Earth, "How long, O Lord, Holy and True?"—still joins (according to Dante's beautiful tradition), in the Lord's Prayer, only modified of course by his knowledge of things by us at present inconceivable and unutterable.

In the concluding Collect all these our instinctive aspirations are summed up, sealed and sanctioned, in that we are ordered to present them to God in express thanksgiving and prayer. "The spirits of them that have departed hence in the Lord," are not dead, but live with Him: "the souls of the faithful, after they are delivered from the burden of the flesh," are not in senseless slumber, but "in joy and felicity." They are still our brethren, and we theirs: as such we are to give thanks for them, and to pray with them that His Kingdom may fully come: our bliss is theirs, and theirs is ours : as Time fails and Eternity comes on, we are still drawing nearer to them and they to us. Such is our thanksgiving for them and for ourselves; and by St. John's Revelation, we know that a door has been opened in Heaven, and voices have come out to signify that in all this we are joining faintly but truly in the services which they in their separate estate are permitted to offer.

Finally ; in a lower key, as beseems frail sinners yet on their trial, "we meekly beseech" our Common Father to save us from forfeiting our blessed Communion, for which we have been thanking Him, with our brethren out of sight. We do not pray that it may be restored, for all along, our acknowledgment has been, that their departure was no interruption to it ; and this very Collect, as is the way of God's heavenly music, repeats the notes with which the Office began : our Lord's own saying, "I am the Resurrection," &c. ; and St. Paul's assurance, equivalent to that of Job, "Sorrow not as the rest who have no hope ; for. . . . them that sleep in Jesus shall God bring with Him," i.e. "As we shall see Him, so shall we also see them, with these very eyes of ours." But what we *do* pray for is, that that most assured meeting may be blessed : that when this grave is opened, and we again meet him whom we have laid there, it may be with mutual joy, and not with grief.

And as this prayer expresses fear and trembling

for ourselves, so the clause in it, which speaks of the Departed is purposely so framed as to express no kind of assurance. I question not that before now many a loving enthusiastic heart has almost felt a shock of disappointment, as it was uttered, " We meekly beseech Thee .... that we may rest in Him, as our hope is this our brother doth." But when we come to consider it, is there anywhere, even iñ the whole Prayer-book, a clause more full-fraught with Wisdom and Charity ? It is indeed the key to the construction of the whole Office. All along, the high and joyful sayings, seeing that they are put into the mouth of mortal man, who cannot read the heart, are to be understood as utterances of sincere Hope, not of opinion, much less of absolute certainty, so far as regards the individual. It is the condition of our earthly being. Higher than this we dare not go, even in the case of one who may appear to us, and to all, to have led the most saintly life : and lower than this, i.e. to the exclusion of all Hope, still less, if possible, may we venture, knowing our Lord's Almightiness and Mercy, and how He can act on the Spirit of Man, if so it please Him, in a moment of time. Only in very extreme cases indeed, where the providential signs are such that no serious person can resist them—such cases as could not well be provided for beforehand under any system of discipline, and which therefore must be met, as they arise, under episcopal correction—could the Church be warranted in declining to express any the slightest hope.

The real difficulty in certain instances does not arise from that saying, nor from anything else in the special wording of the office, but from the fact that the whole of it, both what is said and what is done, from beginning to end, implies that we are dealing with members of Christ's Body; which the Rubric also virtually affirms by excluding the unbaptized and excommunicate. In the total abeyance of our Lord's discipline, it is impossible not to see that the spirit and meaning of that Rubric, as of large portions of the Bible and Prayer-book, is daily and hourly disregarded, and the Burial Service, in common with many other services, (not of course intentionally,) profaned. This, I conceive, especially as regards the Holy Eucharist, is a topic which must unavoidably insert itself into any full discussion of what is called the Burial Question. If it seem to the Governors of our Church (as is most likely) unapproachable at present, I shall be thankful to hear that things remain as they are, only with a generally received understanding that all equitable allowance will be made for the clergy in the rare and frightful cases above alluded to.

*Jan.*, 1854.

# LETTER CXXIII.

## ON THE RITUAL OF THE CHURCH OF ENGLAND[*].

MY DEAR ——,

I have heard something of a proposal to move Convocation, in support of the Bishop of London's expected effort, to obtain a Royal Commission for dealing with an important portion of the Prayer-book. Will you allow me to lay before you the grounds, or a few of them, of the very serious misgiving with which I should regard any such endeavour?

It seems to me perfectly suicidal at present for the lovers of the Church to be opening the door to Parliamentary interference with spiritual matters; unless, indeed, they have made up their minds that the present state of things is so intolerable, that the most religious course is that which will most surely separate us from the State. For it is too evident that the rising Liberalism of the day, being not so much irreligious as anti-dogmatic, while it professes to look with impartial indifference on our several

---

[*] "I hope this [letter which appeared in 'the Literary Churchman'] is more known and considered, especially at this time, than I fear it is. It is written in such an admirable spirit, and with so much clearness and cogency, that one might hope it might furnish a useful guide to the clergy, and allay somewhat of the bitterness, which is so much to be lamented in the manner of waging the present controversy." —*Coleridge's Memoir of J. Keble, p.* 527, *First Edition.*

schools and sections, yet has no objection to play
them one against another for the purpose of putting
down all distinct and exclusive teaching.  Why do
its professors laugh to scorn all that we say, do, or
feel—as Englishmen, not merely as Churchmen—
touching the abuse of the Royal Supremacy in the
matter of the Judicial Committee ?  Because they
know well, that as things are, the Royal Supremacy
is ultimately the mind and will of the House of
Commons, and that mind and will being on the
whole averse to dogma, they, of course, uphold the
institution which is found to work in the same direction.    Thus  it  was  in  the  Gorham  cause ;  thus it
would  have  been  in  Archdeacon  Denison's,  but  by
a providential accident ; thus, flagrantly, in the deci-
sions on behalf of the Essayists and of Dr. Colenso.
Now to these opponents of definite doctrine there
can be no greater encouragement than to find a set
of religious men, working their work, as against those
who are eminently men of dogma—upholders of the
Prayer-book, because of its primitive character.    The
fact was not lost upon them, you may be sure, that
the other day, when there seemed to be a chance
of bringing earnest Churchmen to agree in seeking
redress for the great grievance touching Appeals of
Doctrine, the demur and difficulty and failure was
mainly due to those, to whom the Gorham decision
had been most welcome.    Nor will it lightly be
forgotten, that the " Record" evinced as much zeal

at least, in baffling and discrediting the Bishop of Capetown's work for the Church of Natal, and all his synodical action, as ever it had done in warning men against the rationalism, which called him out. Support from that quarter to Bishop Tait's threatened application was only what might have been expected, and Erastians might reckon on it, as no doubt they do, very confidently. But that you, my dear ——, and persons sympathizing with you, should be found in co-operation with them, this is so far beyond what the Innovators could reasonably have looked for, that it will multiply their number perhaps by tens, and their hopes and energies by thousands; and in the same proportion will discourage and confound the resistance of those, who, loving as you do the Faith and the Church, regard the preservation of the Prayer-book in all material points as essential to the maintenance of both among us. For it will go near to destroy all chance of successfully resisting a Parliamentary revision of the Prayer-book. I say, "a *Parliamentary* revision;" for a Royal Commission, to be effectual, cannot end in anything else. A Royal Commission, of course, must be a Government measure. Now I do not suppose that the present Government, as a body, any more than either or both Houses of Parliament, are themselves violently disposed to such an undertaking; some of them, I believe, would deprecate it with all their hearts. But should any considerable number of sober and earnest

Churchmen unite with the Puritans and Erastians in asking for it, it would be immeasurably harder for such recusants to maintain their position ; and the holiest things would too probably have to be laid, as it were, on the table of the House of Commons, how to be treated, who can say ? At any rate, I would not willingly bear the least part in the responsibility of such a thing.

But you will say, " It is *Convocation* which we wish to address, and that with the view of obviating the apprehended intrusion of Parliament." A dangerous policy, though one were ever so sure of the goodness and wisdom of the proposed enactment. The Church, so calling in an alien power to interfere with spiritual laws, will find itself by-and-by like the horse in Æsop's fable, unable to shake off its rider.   To-day, at your request, the State new-models your Ritual ; to-morrow, at the request of some one else, or of its own free judgment, it will be new-modelling your Creeds and Prayers.  Significant notice was given of this tendency even in the course of a late transaction, which in some respects looked like an instance of deference to Church authority.   It being suggested that the Bill for altering the Form of Clerical Subscription should follow the constitutional precedent of the Act of Uniformity, by reciting in its Preamble, That the said Form had been previously approved by Convocation ; the minister who had the charge of the Bill would by no means allow it, " lest it should countenance the idea that the assent of Convocation was necessary ;" the idea, in which we have been instructed, among others, by our Master Hooker, that, assuming Church and State to be co-extensive, " the Parliament of England *with the Convocation thereto annexed,*" is the sole and sufficient authority for Church legislation among us.  And more, to this same notion we solemnly pledged ourselves according to law, as many as have been ordained Priests, when we promised " so to minister the Doctrine and Discipline of Christ, as *this Church* and Realm hath received the same," not " as the Realm" alone, which Sir G. Grey's argument would imply.  Such a hint from those who now govern ought surely to make us slow in inviting State interference, and in familiarising Parliament with the idea of it, except in very urgent necessity.

But are we at all sure of the wisdom and religiousness of the measure itself, so keenly pressed upon us ?  I will try to state the case as briefly and fairly as I can.  The Anglican portion of Christ's Church, having to review her Canons and Formularies, first in the sixteenth, and afterwards in the seventeenth century, when she came to deal with the vital doctrine of Christ, present and received, in the Holy Eucharist, was providentially guided so to arrange her sayings, and order her symbolical acts, as to maintain, in common with all Christendom for 1500 years, the reality both of the Presence and

of the Sacrifice, while yet, in view of gross errors
recently prevailing, she warned us against all coarse
and earthly interpretations of either.

Thus, on the one hand, under the influence of
Queen Elizabeth, were revived some particulars in
the ceremonial, which had been discontinued in King
Edward's reign ; being such as would most distinctly invite acts of faith and adoration due to
that Holy Mystery (which ceremonies it is now proposed to suppress) ; and, on the other hand, after
the Restoration, while the Church retained the
Rubric in question, and added here and there
other enactments of the same sort, she revived also
from King Edward's second book, the Admonition,
which now stands at the end of her Communion
Office ; thus, unequivocally and once for all, reject-
ing all carnal glosses, whether brought from Italy
or Germany ; while she accepted, in the highest
possible sense, the old Liturgical tenet of the Real
Presence.

Upon this and no other footing did the Church
of England providentially settle herself then ; on
the same and no other has she continued ever
since.   To this every one of her Priests is impli-
citly pledged by the promise already quoted from
the Ordinal.   For since the second Act of Uniformity, this Church and Realm have at no time
joined in any legislative Act, excepting that above
mentioned, relating to Subscription, in the present

year; which, touching only the Form of Subscription, not the matter subscribed to, left both doctrine and ritual unaltered. So far, instead of innovating on the terms of 1662, it was more like a re-enactment of them. And yet even that step was regarded by many with grave doubt, as lending a sanction to unconstitutional interference. A Parliament of all religions, or of none, claiming a voice on the internal arrangements of one particular denomination!

But if *that* was questionable, *this* is simply intolerable. It professes indeed to meddle with one rubric only, but it involves the same prerogative over all; and that which it specifies is one of the most important and comprehensive, bearing directly on one vital doctrine, and through that, as theologians know, upon the whole creed of the Church. And, what is more, those who promote the movement, openly avow that their object is thus comprehensive. The document bearing the respectable names of Mr. Birks, Mr. Ryle, and others, and urging the change of the Rubric by mere statute, grounds itself upon no minor inconveniences, such as alleged unpopularity and danger of riot here and there. They quietly allege that the Bishop of London's scheme, for a Declaration Act, suppressing the usages in question, is necessary to prevent "the Romanistic system" from extending itself, until it is at length allowed unrestricted development in the Church. They say in effect, "such and such religious obser-

vances and doctrines, which, in our private judgment
are wrong and mischievous, stand, however, under
the direct sanction of the Law, and are in a way
to become popular, and be generally received : be
so kind as to pass an act for putting them down."
Well, of course those gentlemen are free, as all are in
this country, to agitate for this, or any other change
of the law.   But there are two things noticeable
in their mode of agitation, unlikely to recommend
it to calm and far-sighted Churchmen.   1. That
the matter being so sacred, so entirely of Ecclesiastical cognizance, they surrender it by preference
into the hands of such a body as our House of
Commons.   2. That they frankly own their purpose
to be, not simply reformation of that one Rubric,
but the discomfiture at all points of a rival section
in the Church.

It is well, perhaps, that they have declared themselves so openly ; it may put many on their guard,
who might otherwise have supported them, at least
passively, as not liking the special usages complained
of, or as fearful of their being revived, when they
would cause disturbance.   Whoever, after this their
plain speaking, shall join in their movement, must
be aware, that he is committing himself to a one-
sided policy, which, ultimately displacing those who
are called Tractarians or the like, will quite over-
throw the sort of equilibrium which for many years
has providentially subsisted among us.   If any one

doubt this, let him only consider what the legal effect of such a change would have been, had it taken place before the prosecutions of Archdeacon Denison here, and Bishop Forbes in Scotland; with how much more show of reason it might have been argued that the Real Presence, as held in the rest of Christendom, had been unequivocally disavowed among us. And if we look beyond our own country, as surely we are bound to do, certain it is that such a decree, not only submitted to, but promoted and solicited by the Convocation of Canterbury, would effectually quench, for the time at least, all the fond hopes of re-union among Christians, which just now appear to be dawning on us in various quarters. For undoubtedly, of all doctrines, that of the Eucharistical Sacrifice is the one, on which, in the eyes both of East and West, our Catholicity would appear most questionable. A hair's breath more of wavering on that point, would seem to them, I fear, an entire forfeiture of our position. As long as we can appeal to our Prayer-book, our Rubrics, and Catechisms, and the dicta of our great accredited Divines, we have wherewithal to confront those, who, on the strength of inadequate expression in some of our Formularies, and still more inadequate obedience to our Rubrics, would impeach our Faith on this point. Just as in regard of the other Sacrament, we indicate our orthodoxy by the plain tenor of our Baptismal Office, in spite of any neglect, misconstruction, or

R

disparagement, with which it may be treated, in this or that school or section of our Body.

In all this, as you will perceive, I take for granted : First—That the usages in question, symbolize, more or less directly, the Doctrines of the Real Presence and Sacrifice. Secondly — That Queen Elizabeth and her advisers in 1558, and the Restorers of the Prayer-book in 1662 ;—i.e. the whole Church of England at those dates respectively ;—are warrant sufficient to allay all suspicion of any special reference in the said symbols to what we disown in the Roman or in the Lutheran doctrine. I may add, that within our own experience, the revivers of those usages have been, and are, found among the most earnest deprecators of Transubstantiation, and of the Pope's Supremacy.

It would seem to follow upon these statements— and I understand that there is a high legal authority for the opinion—that the *onus probandi* lies in this matter upon the many, who practically ignore or slight the usages (of which number I must confess myself to be one), rather than upon the few who have regularly maintained or recently adopted them. I do indeed regret the disregard of that Rubric as a real blemish in our ecclesiastical practice :—a contradiction to our theory, like our almost entire disuse of the Discipline of Jesus Christ, our obligation to which, nevertheless, we formally acknowledge. But as in the latter case, so in this, the time and manner of regaining the old paths must, under our circumstances, be a question of Equity and Charity, not of strict Law alone. I, for one, rejoice whenever and wherever I see that kind of revival successfully and tranquilly accomplished. But the success will be more complete and the satisfaction more perfect, when those who have the work at heart shall have ceased to indulge themselves in invidious comparisons and scornful criticisms on such among their brethren as do not yet see their way to it ; and when, on certain kindred subjects, they have learned to make candid allowance for the difference between our circumstances, and those with a view to which, the Primitive Canons were framed. I allude particularly to the disparaging tone sometimes used in speaking of mid-day Communions, with small consideration, as it seems to me, for the aged and infirm, and others who cannot come early. Again, I cannot but doubt the wisdom of urging all men indiscriminately to be present at our Holy Mysteries : a matter left open, as far as I can see, by the Prayer-book, and in ordering of which it may seem most natural to abide by the Spirit of the ancient Constitutions, which did not willingly permit even the presence of any but Communicants, or those of whom the Clergy had reason to believe that they were in a way to become such. The rather, in that there appears to be some danger of the idea gaining ground, which meets one so often in Roman Catholic books of devotion, of some special, quasi - sacramental, grace, connected with simply assisting devoutly at Mass, over and above that promised to all earnest and faithful prayer.

On these, and all like matters, we may do well, perhaps, to accept the counsel of our Church, in her first Reformed Liturgy, concerning another main point of Christian Discipline[o]. Such as are satisfied with the more modern and plainer Ritual not to be offended with them that adopt the more ornate and symbolical requirements of the Rubric; those, on the other hand, who find comfort and edification in the ceremonies, to bear with their brethren who for various reasons think best to dispense with them for the present. And so, too, in regard of Communion after a meal, and of encouraging the presence of Non-Communicants, and the like: "to follow and keep the rule of Charity, and every man to be satisfied with his own conscience, not judging other men's minds or consciences, whereas he hath no warrant of God's word to the same."

Believe me, dear ——, with great respect, very sincerely yours,

J. KEBLE.

*December,* 1865.

[o] See the First Liturgy of King Edward VI., on Auricular Confession.

Printed by James Parker and Co., Crown-yard, Oxford.

WORKS by the late REV. JOHN KEBLE, M.A., (continued).

THE PSALTER, or PSALMS of DAVID in English
Verse. Adapted to Tunes in common use. Fourth
Edition. Uniform with the Fcap. Edition of the
"Christian Year." Large Fcap. 8vo., on Toned Paper,
cloth, price 6s.

VILLAGE SERMONS ON THE BAPTISMAL SER-
VICE. 8vo., cloth, 5s.

*Lately reprinted.*

"THE STATE IN ITS RELATIONS WITH THE
CHURCH :" A Paper reprinted from the " British
Critic," October, 1839. WITH A PREFACE BY THE
REV. H. P. LIDDON. 8vo., sewed, 2s. 6d.

ON EUCHARISTICAL ADORATION. Third Edition.
WITH CONSIDERATIONS SUGGESTED BY A LATE
PASTORAL LETTER (1858) ON THE DOCTRINE OF THE
MOST HOLY EUCHARIST. 8vo., cloth, 6s.—*Cheap Edition*,
(the Fourth,) 24mo., 2s.

AN ARGUMENT AGAINST REPEALING THE
LAWS WHICH TREAT THE NUPTIAL BOND
AS INDISSOLUBLE. Second Edition, 8vo., 1s.

SUNDAY LESSONS. THE PRINCIPLE OF SELEC-
TION. Being No. XIII. of "Tracts for the Times."
8vo., 6d.

OXFORD and LONDON : JAMES PARKER and Co.

ON THE MYSTICISM ATTRIBUTED TO THE EARLY FATHERS OF THE CHURCH. Being No. LXXXIX. of "Tracts for the Times." 8vo., sewed, 3s. 6d.

THE CHRISTIAN YEAR: THOUGHTS IN VERSE FOR THE SUNDAYS AND HOLYDAYS THROUGHOUT THE YEAR. *Facsimile of the First Edition.* 2 vols., 12mo., cloth, 7s. 6d.

*The following Works may still be obtained.*

THE CHRISTIAN YEAR. In Fcap. 8vo., cloth, 7s. 6d.; 24mo., cloth, 6s.; 32mo., cloth, 3s. 6d.; *Cheap Edition*, cloth, 1s. 6d.

LYRA INNOCENTIUM: THOUGHTS IN VERSE ON CHRISTIAN CHILDREN, THEIR WAYS, AND THEIR PRIVILEGES. Fcap. 8vo., cloth, 7s. 6d.; *Cheap Edition*, cloth, 1s. 6d.

THE LIFE OF THOMAS WILSON, D.D., Lord Bishop of Sodor and Man. Compiled chiefly from Original Documents. In Two Parts. 8vo., cloth, 21s.

OXFORD and LONDON: JAMES PARKER and CO.